URBAN RENEWAL

Bonanza of the
Real Estate Business

URBAN RENEWAL

Bonanza of the
Real Estate Business

Daniel S. Berman

PRENTICE-HALL, INC.   Englewood Cliffs, N.J.

Prentice-Hall International, Inc., London
Prentice-Hall of Australia, Pty. Ltd., Sydney
Prentice-Hall of Canada, Ltd., Toronto
Prentice-Hall of India Private Ltd., New Delhi
Prentice-Hall of Japan, Inc., Tokyo

Library of Congress
Catalog Card Number: 72–80651

This publication is designed to provide
accurate and authoritative information
with regard to the subject matter covered.
It is sold with the understanding that the
publisher is not engaged in rendering legal,
accounting, or other professional advice.
If legal advice or other expert assistance
is required, the services of a competent
professional person should be sought.

... From a Declaration of Principles jointly
adopted by a Committee of the American Bar
Association and a Committee of Publishers
and Associations

Printed in the United States of America
13–939231–9 B&P

To my father, Joseph Berman,
whose early guidance and encouragement
grow more important each year

ABOUT THE AUTHOR

Daniel S. Berman conducts a workshop on Urban Renewal at New York University's Graduate Real Estate Institute. During the past twenty five years, he has lectured on real estate law before housing, building, banking, and trade organizations. Brokers, builders, and other real estate professionals from all over the country have attended his seminars and workshops on the tax aspects of real estate, syndicates, and condominiums. Mr. Berman is a New York attorney, and a member of the Real Estate Board of New York, the National Association of Home Builders, and the Long Island and Westchester Builders Institutes.

WHAT THIS BOOK WILL DO FOR YOU

If you live in almost any city in the United States today, the chances are that within a few minutes' drive from your home or office there is available in the downtown center of your city a large, undeveloped parcel of real estate located in the very heart of your community which you, or a group of investors which you form, can purchase at a price substantially below the cost to the United States Government.

"But," you say, "I've heard all about Urban Renewal—you have to have political influence to get that land." Perhaps you also will say "Yes, I know, that land has been sitting there for years. The reason nobody wants to buy it, even at a discount, is because it is located in such a blighted neighborhood you can't give it away."

Neither of these frequently voiced objections is true. In most cases, you do not have to be politically well connected to get involved in the Urban Renewal program. When you read the first chapter of this book, you will see exactly why the Urban Renewal people need you more than you need the piece of land. Nothing moves in the Urban Renewal program until a private developer or a community group decides it wants to buy the piece of land and build on it.

So, you see, the land is available to almost anyone with a sincere interest in it. And, as a matter of fact, mortgage financing guaranteed by a United States Government agency offering loans of up to 103% (in special cases) are available to help put the deal together.

"Yes," you say, "but you haven't overcome my argument that this property is in such a blighted area you can't give it away." As to this, it is important to note that today's blighted neighborhood can become tomorrow's most desirable neighborhood, providing the developer has the imagination and skill to see its proper use, with the old, dilapidated buildings removed and with new landscaping, new tenants and new structures.

Let us remember that Georgetown, in Washington, D. C. was a slum some years ago, and that some of the better neighborhoods in Philadelphia were at one time slums; that Lincoln Center and the Coliseum, in New York City, were built on Urban Renewal land.

Before you criticize the Urban Renewal parcel as a slum, remember how close it is to the center of town; how much good transportation serves the area; how cheaply you can buy it; and how good the financing will be.

Urban Renewal land is available for apartments, both low income and luxury; for shopping centers; for department stores; for downtown parking; for office buildings; for hotels and motels; for sports stadiums; for retail stores; and for medical buildings and hospitals. You name the use—I'll find for you somewhere within the boundaries of this large country in one or more of the 2,000 to 3,000 Urban Renewal sites now located throughout the country, a site specifically ear-marked for your purpose.

The book simply deals with getting something modern built on under-utilized and blighted sites. The sites are there and the financing is there. The heartaches and troubles are there, too. To get started, you need the initiative and the imagination; to finish, you must have the know-how to work around the obstacles.

It is the purpose of this book to lead you through the Urban Renewal program, step by step, so that you will see for yourself how others have come to these downtown blighted sites and have found in them a bonanza. It is my hope that this book will serve as a guide for you, too, and that it will also warn you of some of the major pitfalls that others have experienced, so that you will be able to avoid them.

Do not let the size of the job deter you, nor its difficulty. Remember, you need only build one successful job in a lifetime to find retirement income for yourself and an estate for your heirs.

WHAT IS URBAN RENEWAL?

As set forth in this book, Urban Renewal involves the process by which our Government condemns and appropriates with public funds urban land, usually in the older sections of the city, which is blighted. The Government, through a local community agency, then offers to re-sell the land to developers or local community groups who agree to build on the cleared land site a new project in accordance with the "Urban Renewal Plan."

The "Plan," which is printed in brochure or pamphlet form, is the result of careful study both by the community and a group of professionals called Urban Planners.

You, or a group formed by you, can purchase this land at a price substantially below the cost of the land to the Government, in most cases. To aid you in re-developing this land, special financing programs are usually available.

This book tells you how to find an Urban Renewal site suitable for your particular project, how to buy that site, how to finance the construction, how to get a permanent mortgage, and how to get the tax benefits and profits which the program offers. If you are a community agency called a "non-profit sponsor," the book will tell you how to get your project started and how to speed it up by cutting down on the red tape.

Those are the facets of Urban Renewal which are covered in this book. There are also other important facets which I hardly need mention: the community and social benefits. Urban Renewal upgrades the physical appearance of urban centers, promotes the building of new streets and schools, and attracts new businesses and jobs. It also enhances the social environment of the residents, by encouraging the installation of social agencies and a whole group of community programs and services aimed at improving the social environment of the community and uplifting its residents.

CONTENTS

and Other Controls . Local Code Compliance . Local General Contractor? . Amend the Urban Renewal Plan? . Major or Minor Plan Change?

Other Problems . Extra Costs . Co-ordination . Timing of Supporting Facilities . Mortgages . Is There a Market? . Assembling the Team . Buying Your Land . Design Competitions . The Price Is "Too Good" . Sponsors . Tips and Warnings for Sponsors . Open Competitive Disposition . Examining the Plan . Unusual Title Problems . Safeguards . Overcoming the Problems . Other Available Data . Overcoming Restrictions . Financing and Restrictions . Your Architect . Soil Conditions . Utilities—Sewers—Roads . Your Rights Against the LPA . Redeveloper's Statement . Your Deposit or Bond . Who Shall Take Title? . The Road Map—Step by Step . What to Do While You Wait? . The License to Enter the Land . Time to Perform . Piecemeal Performance . Excuses for Non-Performance . Buying Versus Renting . Comparing the Lease with a Purchase . Leasehold Carrying Charges . Covenants Running with the Land . Fulfillment of Conditions . No Unnecessary Burdens . LPA's Duties . Anti-Speculation Provisions . Some Required Exceptions . Project Commencement Date . How Much Down? . Cash Versus Bonds . Terms of Bond . Off-Site Improvements . Recordable Proof of Performance . What Does Your Lender Say? . Checklist

Conventional Financing and How It Is Done . Equity Financing—The Key . Site Location . Buying the Land "Right" . Tax Considerations on Taking Title . Hunting for a Conventional Mortgage . Construction Money Against the Permanent Loan . And Now Construction Starts . Timing Your Advances . Using Subs to Finance Your Job . Commitment for Variable Amounts of Mortgage Loans . Effect of Money Shortage . Renting . The Conventional Timetable . Why Push for the Highest Mortgage? . Leverage at Work . Developing an FHA Apartment Job . Why FHA at All, Then? . FHA Site Approval . Sounding Out FHA . Mini-

or rejection . What Your Form 2012 Reveals . Form 2013
(Your Loan Insurance Application) . Some Form 2013
Details . The Dilemma of Non-Residential Income . Gross
Income Calculations on Form 2013 . Enough Income to
Service Your Debt . Estimating Operating Cost Figures .
Do Forms 2012 and 2013 Together . Vacancy Allowances .
Real Estate Tax Estimates . The Key Figure on Form 2013
. Carrying Charges During Construction . Legal and
Organizational Expenses . How Much Equity Will You Need?
. The Income Available for Debt Service "Trap" . A Way
Out on § 220 . Re-Working a Close Set of Figures . Form
2013 Requires Exhibits . Various Addenda to Form 2013
(Including Form 2435) . Form 2419 (Replacement Reserves)
. Getting Your Tentative Commitment . The Initial Closing
. Why a "Dry Run" Is Vital to Your Closing

Chapter I

WHY GET INVOLVED IN URBAN RENEWAL?

Almost this entire Volume is devoted to the techniques of processing paper through many governmental agencies and explaining in detail how to overcome the important problems and cut your way through tons of red tape. So it is important to ask ourselves at the very beginning--why get involved at all? True, a number of foundations and social agencies have gone into the program purely to "do good" for the community, but the aim of this book is to show you how to make money out of the program. The financial opportunities are so good that no intelligent businessman who is in the building, real estate or construction industries can afford to overlook them.

The Size of the Program
and the Money Involved

Jim Scheuer, one of the early "urban renewers," pointed out the size of the program years ago when the program was much smaller than it is today. Mr. Scheuer, in a Columbia Law Review article (June 1962), said:

The number of acres covered by projects in earlier stages of formulation exceeds the 291,000 acres contained in the city borders of Los Angeles, our largest city in area. Indeed, in terms of acreage, the redevelopment program will ultimately encompass an area of metropolitan land comparable to the total area of the ten largest cities in the United States. If this land is successfully populated, in the 1960's there will be an impact on life in the United States—similar to that caused by the migration to suburbia, exurbia, and beyond during the 1940's and 1950's—caused by the return of a significant fraction of the total population to residence in the redeveloped central cities.

The land sales under the program will exceed in total dollars the amounts received in any of the major dispositions of the public domain in our history. In the next ten years alone the total value of the land that will be available for sale under the Urban Renewal Program should exceed $2 billion, a sum which, even allowing for inflation, far exceeds the $10 million involved in the Gadsten purchase, the $15 million price of the Louisana Purchase, or even the $414,200,000 received from all the sales of public land from 1785 to 1956.

The enormity of the land disposition phase of the Urban Renewal program has been overlooked in large part because disposition has barely started. As of December of 1961 only 3,806 acres (just 12% of the acreage then into advanced planning) had actually been disposed of for a total of $173,400,000. Indeed, the first land disposition was in 1952 and the first completion of the disposition phase in any Urban Renewal project did not occur until 1955. The importance of this phase has also been obscured in part because those acres already disposed of were contained in 240 widely scattered projects.

1968's $5 Billion Housing Bill

In spite of an economy drive, Congress went along with the Johnson Administration's 1968 request for the largest housing bill in history. Totaling $5. 3 billion over the first three years, the bill aimed at building or rehabilitating 26, 000, 000 housing units over a ten-year span, with a number of new concepts. Special programs to encourage home ownership among the poor, rent subsidies for the poor, new programs for loans to mobile and vacation homes, a program for guaranteeing financing on "new towns" and a technique

2

of forming partnerships or joint ventures between a government corporation (like "Comsat") were among the innovations included in what was probably the most important housing statute since Taft's post-World War II Urban Renewal Laws.

Removing 26,000,000 sub-standard units over the next ten years, an average of over 2-1/2 million units a year, is bound to have an impact on the market, especially in view of the fact that the entire private market has not built as many as 2-1/2 million homes in any recent year. While it is too early to predict how enthusiastically Congress or ensuing administrations will fund this program, it is impossible to overlook the importance of a program that aims at providing home ownership for the first time in this country's history to families in the $6,000 and $7,000 income brackets.

Some Misconceptions About Urban Renewal

Many consultants and builders think about Urban Renewal only in terms of large projects. This is not true. Seventy percent of the cities participating in the Urban Renewal program have populations of less than 50,000. These smaller cities have small, one-family home projects in mind in most cases. Development is done by local builders. The big jumbo projects get the major portion of our attention. But do not overlook the fact that 70% of the program is in cities with less than 50,000 people. In those smaller cities, over 140,000 units were scheduled, on some 4,700 acres, with a substantial portion allocated for smaller multi-family units and single-family home sales.

No Zoning Problems

Most Urban Renewal projects solve your zoning and land use problems before you buy. There is no need for re-zoning; there is no battle over how many apartments should be allocated to the acre, because these decisions have been made and are known in advance. They are outlined in writing in the Urban Renewal plan. Also, there is no doubt about the kind of mortgage commitment that will be available to you (if you are going to use one of the FHA programs). Merely by asking the local FHA office or Local Public Agency (LPA), you can find out in advance the amount of the mortgage that will be available.

No Market Study Needed

The market demand has been studied by both the Local Public Agency and the FHA for the specific kind and quantity of housing contemplated. Of course, you will want to make your own decision on the validity of the marketing contentions. You may run your own marketing survey aside from the FHA's—although much preliminary information can be found without spending a dime on research—just by walking into the local renewal office. You'll see what information is available and how to get it.

Roads and Utilities Supplied

Off-site improvements are kept to a minimum and most of them are paid for by the local municipality (with federal funds). The Urban Renewal plan lays out, in most cases, a road-building and utility installation program to be paid for by one of the government agencies, thus eliminating these headaches and costs from the builder's dilemna. Gone is the need for street and paving bonds.

A Friend at City Hall

Also, if you take on an Urban Renewal job, don't battle with City Hall—the local municipality should be on your side. Indeed, a special agency, the Local Public Agency (abbreviated from here on as the LPA), has been established at a local level to see that the Urban Renewal program succeeds. The very jobs and prestige of this civic organization, and its entire staff, depend upon helping you get your job built.

These people are on your side and they will go with you from agency to agency to help you get clearance. Their contacts at a local level should be excellent. Instead of having to fight every city agency, you will find an important agency on your side to take up the cudgels with those who seek to slow down or interfere with your success.

You Know in Advance

If you read the Urban Renewal plan carefully—the plan which is going to affect your project—not only will you be able to discover what is required of you and what is required of the municipality, but you will be told in advance what is going to happen to the neighboring land. You can visualize the entire project from the beginning—and sell the fact that you are going to be across the street from a new concert hall, a civic center, or whatever.

Timing

Timing is the key problem in Urban Renewal. Not only will you be on the job longer (because it is larger than most jobs that you will do), but your cash will be in longer and you will have to put it up earlier. It is wise to budget and plan for these facts in advance.

The Urban Renewal builder is required to put up the cost of the land at the time he purchases it, and most governmentally financed jobs will not permit you to raise your working capital by using the customers' sales deposits. So, you are going to have to sink your own money into the job and it will be in longer, because of the red tape which we will discuss later.

Because you contact the governmental agency earlier in Urban Renewal than in regular building, the timing seems to be longer than it really is. In a conventional, non-Renewal job, you might spend a year and one-half or two years between the time you first locate a parcel to the time you arrange for the financing of the land, get it re-zoned, file your plans, get them approved, and make arrangements for the streets, the utilities and the bonding thereof. In an Urban Renewal job, all of this preliminary work will have been done before you walk into the picture so that, after reading your plan and contacting the agency, you will get started as soon as you buy. You will have other problems, true, but you will also save some preliminary motions.

On the other hand, some of the things you want to do in Urban Renewal take longer than they would in a private job. If you want changes in plans or specifications, you are going to have to run them through all the usual government agencies, plus a raft of specialized ones that deal only with Urban Renewal. In other words, if you want to change the plans from those set forth in the Urban Renewal plan, not only will you have to get local Building Department approval, but you may require the consent of various state and federal agencies, including the LPA, the City Council,

Regional Headquarters of HUD, possibly National Headquarters of HUD, etc., depending on whether the plan changes are "major" or "minor."

Learn the Procedures

Leon Weiner, N. A. H. B. President, who has built many Urban Renewal jobs, had this to say:

> The most important thing about going into Renewal is to understand that it involves a great deal of relationship with the LPA and the city government. The builder must learn the procedures, just as we had to learn how to handle these things in the early days of FHA, or even in conventional financing.

> Urban Renewal is a business opportunity, but because of the public planning involved, there is a concern for the program, design and execution which frequently requires a lot more of the public relations aspect.

The Financial Benefits (or How to Make Money In Urban Renewal)

When I asked one developer why he got involved in Urban Renewal in the first place, instead of answering, he asked me a question: "Where else can I get to build and own $1 million worth of real estate with as little as $30,000 of my own cash?" That, succinctly sums up the attitude of the professional.

Let us look in greater detail at some of the benefits of the Urban Renewal program:

1. Leverage

Since it is possible to do an Urban Renewal job with as little as a 3% cash investment, the program offers you a chance at tremendous leverage. How else could you hope to own $1 million worth of real estate with a $30,000 investment; $10 million worth of real estate with a $300,000 investment? What other way could a builder buy several million dollars worth of rent roll with little or no cash of his own? Where else is it possible to buy such a huge hedge against inflation—such an opportunity to get 40-year mortgage financing based on today's construction costs? Where else is there an opportunity to buy millions of dollars of downtown land written down by federal and local governments, with very little cash of your own?

2. Tax Benefits

Interest and taxes, during the construction period, can be written off against current taxable income. Upper-bracket taxpayers are fascinated by this. Corporations get benefits exceeding 50% (when federal and state rates are combined) and upper-bracket individuals find that 70 cents on the dollar can be written off against current income taxes. Not only does the Urban Renewal program offer an opportunity for you to own large projects with an infinitesimal cash investment, but most of your equity investment can be written off very quickly against payments that would otherwise be due to the tax collector. In other words, even the 3% cash you must put in is supplied indirectly by a subsidy from the tax collector.

Let us assume that you start with a $300,000 investment in a $10 million project and that you, the investor, are an individual in the 70% tax bracket. If the $300,000 goes in over several years, and if you stay in the 70% tax bracket, 70 cents on the dollar will come out of the tax collector's pocket—only 30 cents out of yours. This can leave you with as little as $90,000 in the job, after deducting tax savings up to $110,000. You would then be in the position of owning a $10 million job on a $90,000 cash investment.

Suppose, however, you are not in the 70% tax bracket—suppose you are a young builder trying to get started. It should not be too hard to find an upper-bracket taxpayer who will act as a silent partner investor—who is in the 70% tax bracket. Such an investor will usually be willing to put up the whole $300,000, in exchange for part of the deal plus a piece of the tax deduction. More about that later. At this point, all we want to do is to show you that the income tax picture in Urban Renewal is the factor that puts a gleam in the eyes of upper-bracket taxpayers. Even if you yourself are not an upper-bracket taxpayer, you should find it easy to locate a partner who welcomes those tax deductions, in exchange for putting up the cash "front money."

3. A Captive Market

Many building products companies have financed Urban Renewal projects as partners of builders and realtors to permit them to test new markets for their products. True, these nationally known organizations would not have gone into the program merely to sell their products--they certainly wanted the other benefits outlined in this book. But, finding a captive market for substantial amounts of their building materials has been a major incentive to such organizations as Alcoa and Reynolds and U. S. Gypsum. Other building products groups that have done financing include such companies as Armstrong Cork, The American Plywood Association and others.

In some cases, real estate management firms, architects, lawyers and contracting organizations have put together Urban Renewal programs for the fees, the management prerequisites and other benefits.

Suppose, for example, you are a real estate management firm and that you are not able to find an upper-bracket taxpayer to put up the $300,000 involved in our hypothetical $10 million deal. While real estate management and leasing commissions vary from one part of the country to another, if your deal just breaks even and pays no cash return whatsoever, you may find the $50,000 to $75,000 of annual management fees, leasing and insurance commissions a pretty good return on your $300,000 investment--especially if there are tax benefits coupled with it.

If principals of your organization are in the 50% tax bracket, and if $300,000 of investment can be written off over the first few years in the form of deductible interest and tax charges, your money can come back in two years—leaving you thereafter $50,000 to $75,000 of annual fees coming in on no investment at all.

4. Retail and Commercial Space

FHA § 220 mortgages now permit the building of retail store areas "incidental" to a large apartment project in Urban Renewal. This can mean a 40-year mortgage for you on those stores. Even if you wish to forego the benefits of 40-year FHA financing, conventional financing may be available for the retail store areas. Many Urban Renewal projects include land for retail store or office use adjacent to the housing uses. While both the commercial

8

and residential sites are vacant, neither one seems to have any great attractiveness. However, once the apartment houses are completed, the adjacent commercial land offers a wonderful opportunity at capital appreciation. If you buy both sites, merely breaking even on the apartment house site may offer an opportunity of a 10,000% return on the commercial site.

5. The Build-up of Mortgage Amortization

Let us again look at our hypothetical $10 million project. Let us assume a 40-year, self-liquidating FHA § 220 mortgage. In 40 years you will own $10 million worth of real estate free and clear. It is true that 40 years is a long time to wait. However, in 20 years you will have amortized slightly less than $4 million of that mortgage; in 10 years, almost $1-1/2 million. Your mortgage equity builds up pretty quickly when you are dealing with eight-figure mortgages, and re-financing is always worth thinking about once the job is built and rented.

In fact, many builders overlook the importance of mortgage amortization in their early planning. It is not hard to understand why this is so. To a builder in the process of working like the devil to build and rent, it is hard to visualize that 10 to 20 years from now his project may be worth substantially more money—his room rentals will seem very low and he may have a waiting list of tenants.

Remember though that many builders who ran away from their § 608 projects after World War II—happy to sell for a series of notes—wish that they continued to own those very projects. Many of the 1949 and 1950 § 608 projects have been re-financed with conventional mortgages, thus freeing six-figure replacement reserves in cash and permitting subsequent buyers to "mortgage out" once again. Conventional re-financing released FHA rental and other controls.

Bear in mind that the land values of your Urban Renewal project have been substantially written down and are unlikely to fall below the price which you pay. It is equally unlikely that construction costs and replacement costs will fall substantially below today's levels. It is almost impossible to believe that five or ten years after you complete your Urban Renewal project, you will have a harder time finding tenants in your <u>renewed</u> area.

In other words, once the area is renewed and fully rented, tenants form a waiting list to get in. Some examples: the Hyde Park Projects in Chicago, Alcoa's projects in New York. Almost any completed Urban Renewal project will be worth more a few years from now than it is today. If you carefully select your project, your mortgage amortization should be as good as gold. Inflation and mortgage amortization can be worth millions in a single job.

It would seem, then, that the mortgage amortization and leverage benefits may be the biggest bonanza of the entire project. They are more important than even the tax savings in the early years—even though the tax savings will help you get investors. If you cannot lick your lips with anticipation at owning $10 million of real estate, building up your mortgage amortization at an average rate of $250,000 a year, then you do not belong in the real estate business. It only takes one job like this to build a young fortune—and you don't have to wait 40 years to cash in on the benefits.

6. Tax Savings Can Bring 50% Returns on Your Investment

Many upper-bracket investors buy apartment houses merely for their depreciation benefits. Once your project is completed and rented, these benefits offer an opportunity to resell your project at a capital gain. A clear understanding of those tax benefits is also useful in helping you to find investor-partners with "front money" to help get the job off the ground.

Let us examine some of the "pluses" that Urban Renewal offers in the tax-saving field. To begin with, the mortgage amortization problem which usually cripples tax benefits in most apartment projects, is minimized in Urban Renewal projects. The long mortgage and low annual amortization in the early years is less than the depreciation which offsets it. In other words, an Urban Renewal project offers maximum tax shelter. Indeed, this tax shelter is so large in the early years, that the deal should show a cash profit at the same time it is showing a tax loss!

Land costs in Urban Renewal projects generally represent the smallest possible percentage of total job costs—so that non-depreciable land is minimized. Urban Renewal land costs are written down below governmental costs, so that it is entirely possible for an Urban Renewal project to have $20 million worth of bricks sitting on top of $500,000 or $600,000 worth of land. Even better, the construction may be upon <u>leased</u> land rather than <u>owned</u> land.

It would be hard to find a conventionally financed project with such a low percentage of land cost. As we mentioned above, land cost may be eliminated altogether in Urban Renewal projects if the land is leased rather than purchased. Governmental regulations permit such land leasing.

However, let us look at our hypothetical $20 million worth of bricks sitting on top of $500,000 of land. That leaves $20 million worth of depreciable real estate. At a 5% double declining method of depreciation (twice 2-1/2% on a 40-year life) you would have $1 million of depreciation the first year. To a corporation at the 50% state and federal tax brackets, if we assume a $600,000 investment in the project, there would be almost one-half million dollars of tax savings the first year. This represents a return of almost 100% on the investment (even though we have assumed no cash profit, nor any tax benefit from deducting construction taxes or interest, nor any mortgage amortization).

While it is true that the non-deductible mortgage amortization will tend to offset this tax benefit, and while it is further true that double-declining balance depreciation does certainly decline, no matter how you make the computations, you will see that the tax romance of depreciation alone offers huge incentives to upper-bracket taxpayers. Very few taxpayers in the 50%-and-up brackets can find investments that will return their money to them in three to five years just out of tax savings.

In addition to the savings, there are the other benefits: the mortgage amortization, leverage, real estate values, rental appreciation and capital gains possibilities. A married taxpayer reaches the top tax bracket at only $40,000 a year. At his level and up, Urban Renewal makes an attractive investment.

Let us begin to examine some cash return figures.

Returns Can Be Higher Than Projected

FHA programs are planned to limit your return somewhat. Let us examine some of the projected returns and compare them with some <u>actual</u> returns.

The government agencies understand that your "estimated" income and expenses to them are "projections." To a certain extent, some of the expenses shown on those estimates may be cut—particularly if you are a capable manager.

Let us assume that your projected returns show the agency that you expect to make 6% ($18,000 on a $300,000 investment in a $10 million job with $1 million of rents). When can you increase that 6% return?

Vacancies

Ordinarily, you would estimate 7% for vacancies. If your project is well planned and your rental campaign aggressive, you may wind up with vacancies of no more than 2% to 3%. This could mean $50,000 a year more on $1 million of rent. Now your return is $68,000 on $300,000. True, if you "goof" you may have vacancies of higher than 7%—particularly in the early years—but, if you do as well as we estimated, you are now making over 23%.

Management Expenses

Here you should just about break even with the government estimates—but if you are managing many apartments and have your own management organization, you may even shave a half point or even a whole one off your $1 million rent roll. This can mean $5,000 to $10,000 more; now your return can be $78,000 on $300,000 (plus possible insurance commissions, too). You are above 25% on your equity.

Operating Expenses

Efficient managers have been known to shave operating expenses as much as $3 to $6 a room a month. This can mean additional returns of five and six figures on a substantial job; $50,000 added to our previous $78,000 figure brings you above $125,000 on your $300,000. Your figure is now over 40% on equity. True, few jobs turn out this well, but we want to show you where the romance lies and what the possibilities are.

Replacement Reserves

The amounts which the government requires you to put aside in a cash escrow are extremely high on new buildings. The amount allowed for repairs alone should clearly cover your maintenance and most of the small replacements in the early years so that the escrow is all clear profit, if you can get at it. Although you will not be able to pry the cash loose from the escrow during those early years, the cash will become available once you are able to do conventional re-financing and break free of government controls. Each program has its own built-in time limits on re-financing, but cash running to six figures has been released from some of the early FHA multi-family housing projects merely by replacing them with conventional financing. From the tenth year on, this can become a six-figure opportunity to the builder.

Real Estate Tax Estimates

These are estimated as high as possible for the lending agencies—at the same time they are protested and reduced with the local municipality. Five figure savings are possible in large projects.

To Summarize

The opportunities in Urban Renewal profits lie in minimizing your cash investment by re-investing your sponsor's profit and risk allowance (similar to a developer's fee, of 10%). That may cut your cash requirements down to 2% to 3%.

Annual returns running 3 or 4 times the 6% shown on equity are also possible. Those returns depend on your ability to rent up quickly and stay rented. Opportunities may also be found in shaving operating expenses, administration, management and insurance costs, cutting real estate taxes below the estimates—and freeing replacement reserves to the extent they have built up during the early years of operation.

Plus Mortgage Amortization

Finally, do not forget that if the property just breaks even,

13

you are building up an average of $25,000 a year of mortgage amortization on a $1 million project; $250,000 a year on a $10 million project. Add that to your possible cash returns of 25% and up, and do not overlook the tax benefits, and you will see why you do not have to build many Urban Renewal jobs, if you build just one that succeeds.

The "Profit" in "Non-Profit" Housing

Even jobs which you build to re-sell to a co-op group, on which you cannot make more than 6%, offer good cash returns. § 221(d)(3) offers 103% financing (even the working capital is lent) to bona fide non-profit organizations. The program offers a below market interest rate of 3%. Maximum mortgage limits are $12-1/2 million per project, and Congress felt that since the sponsor would be a bona fide non-profit builder such as a church, a labor union, etc., these organizations would have no incentive to "mortgaging out" and could be trusted to undertake building a project which would be socially useful.

The spark in these non-profit housing projects, of course, is supplied by the private developer who knows how to get the project off the ground and who will undertake the long, arduous paper work of clearing the project through FHA. For this, you can earn 6 and 7 figure "builders' fees." FHA carefully investigates, however, to make sure that all the builder is getting out of the deal is the builder's profit, and that the non-profit sponsor really takes over once the job is finished.

However, if you want to build and own, 90% loans are available to "limited dividend" profit-making corporations. Such corporations can be owned by the builder, but the return is, presumably, "limited." On paper, the builder cannot earn more than 6% on his 10% equity. However, since his 10% equity can be part cash and part "sweat" or "builder's fee" which the builder earns and can re-invest in the job, returns may very well go above the 15% margin on actual cash invested. For example, in a limited dividend project costing $2 million ($100,000 land; $1.9 million building) the builder would be permitted to earn a 10% fee on a $1.9 million or $190,000.

If the builder got a $1.8 million mortgage on his $2 million project and if he left his $190,000 builder's fee in the job to offset

14

the $200, 000 paper investment, he would only have $10, 000 of cash in the job. Since he would be allowed a 6% return on his paper equity of $200, 000 (or $12, 000 per year), the $12, 000 a year return would equal 120% per annum on his actual cash equity of $10, 000.

Land Profits Also

For a while § 221(d)(3) offered an opportunity to make a land profit in co-ops in which the builder purchased a piece of land (outside of urban renewal areas), re-zoned it, marked it up, and then sold it to a § 221(d)(3) co-op. Tenant cooperators were interested because they were buying at substantially below market rates, particularly since low interest and small down payments were available. Officially, the FHA has been unwilling to recognize land profits. Admittedly, they do not require cost certification on land; however, by tightening or loosening appraisal practices, local FHA offices have effectively permitted or rejected opportunities for builders to make a land profit if they buy land at substantially below market value, or if they put some work product into the land by getting it re-zoned, etc. You should certainly check out the opportunity to make a land profit any time you get involved in any of the governmentally assisted or guaranteed programs. In some cases, the potential land profit may be the most attractive part of the program.

Whether particular builders will continue doing § 221(d)(3) projects merely for the builder's fee (which ranges up to 10%) without the incentive of a land profit remains to be seen and will depend largely on the competition for the builder's investment dollar and how slow or how fast the building business is moving at a particular time and how anxious particular builders are to make this fee, as well as how much paper work has to be done to get it and what the risks are.

Summarizing the Benefits
of Urban Renewal

Urban Renewal is just beginning to have real impact on the American scene and on the building industry. The hundreds of thousands of acres all across the country which it has taken almost fifteen years to acquire must be disposed of.

Not only are there opportunities in every large city in the United States, but 70% of the program is geared to cities of under 50,000 population.

Urban Renewal offers the imaginative developer an opportunity to capitalize on:

1. Maximum leverage, with equities going down to as little as 3%;

2. Maximum tax shelter, and even an opportunity to use "paper depreciation" tax losses to offset other income;

3. Downtown land already assembled and written down: a unique opportunity to purchase large downtown sites already assembled, pre-zoned and "ready to go";

4. Tax sheltered investment opportunity for non-builders, an attractive package for passive investors who wish to pool their funds with the know-how of skilled building or real estate organizations;

5. Captive markets, a chance to capture large management, insurance, rental, building supply and other markets connected with multi-million dollar projects;

6. Equity buildings of 6 figures and more, a chance to own multi-million dollar housing and commercial projects as a hedge against inflation with maximum loan leverage and minimum investment on your part, coupled with annual mortgage amortization and replacement reserve escrows which alone can build up equities of $1, $10 and $15 million in periods as short as 10 to 20 years—especially as neighborhoods build up and conventional re-financing becomes possible.

In short, to the imaginative, aggressive professional, Urban Renewal offers the opportunity of building your fortune in one, well-conceived, well-managed project. We can think of no other field that offers such unique money-making opportunities to people with know-how and persistence. Even the financing can come from outside, as has been pointed out in the preceding pages. What is required in the Urban Renewal field is persistence and know-how— we cannot stress that too many times.

16

The financing and opportunities must follow—even though you may have limited funds of your own. Never forget that while it is true that the red tape is formidable, both the federal government and the Local Public Agency are behind you 100%—politically as well as socially—and they want to see you succeed. The rest is up to you. Even the equity financing need not be yours—every city contains innumerable upper-bracket investors who would love to join with you for their share of the depreciation.

Chapter II

HOW TO GET STARTED IN URBAN RENEWAL

What It Is and When It Starts

Before taking you step-by-step through the Urban Renewal program, commencing with your first visit to the Local Public Agency and running through your financing and construction problems, it would be well to say a few words about what the Urban Renewal program is—what agencies play a part in it, what an Urban Renewal "plan" is, and what it means to you.

Urban Renewal starts at a local municipal level and, subject to certain federal controls, always remains at a local level, with the responsibility for planning and execution left in local hands. In other words, control is in your home town.

Urban Renewal begins by a local municipality setting up an LPA (Local Public Agency). The major local governing bodies such as the city or village council, hire a man or a staff to come up with a plan to "renew" certain of the city's "blighted" areas as part of an overall renewal of the city.

18

Federal Funds

In general, two-thirds of the funds will come from Washington, with the other third coming from the local municipality. Many states have adopted their own state renewal agency, which will provide 50% of the city's third, leaving the city with only one-sixth in some cases. Even that one-sixth may be in the form of a credit for certain city improvements (such as schools or roads) which cuts the city's extra cash needs to almost zero.

From the initial plans, through the acquisition by condemnation and/or negotiation, to the cost of holding and selling the land, the federal government picks up two-thirds of the tab, with the state and city picking up the other third.

The Costs

A number of costs are involved—if you think about it. First, there is the cost of coming up with the plan; then there is the cost of acquiring the land and re-locating the people living on it; then there is the loss or "write-down" involved in re-selling the land for the new Urban Renewal use. The sales price is usually only a fraction of the actual acquisition cost. Then there is the cost of administering the program and doing the financing, as well as such costs as building new roadways and schools for the renewed city areas.

Again, behind all these stands the federal government and its various programs with the funds necessary to come up with its portion of the cost.

The Urban Renewal Plan

The product or end result of the early planning is a so-called "Urban Renewal plan." It is a big, thick brochure or folder with many copies printed. The Urban Renewal plan started out in the offices of an Urban Renewal planner (whose fee was paid by the various governmental agencies participating in the program). The planner's initial report was reviewed by the mayor and the local legislative body before and after public hearings in which the local citizenry and organized groups were given an opportunity to object and suggest changes.

19

Finally, after holding local public hearings and going through many local changes, the plan went through city and state agencies (if the state played any part in the program) and then to the United States Department of Housing and Urban Development to eventually reach the state of an approved Urban Renewal plan, which was printed up in brochure form.

Carrying Out the Plan

The duty of carrying out that Urban Renewal plan (i. e., seeing that the land was acquired, the people re-located, the site cleared, and the proposed renewal buildings constructed, financed and rented) was left in the hands of the Local Public Agency. That agency was charged with the duty to select the best people to do each of the jobs called for therein.

By the time you, as a developer or builder, come to the Local Public Agency which has a cleared site for sale or lease, much hard work has already taken place and large sums of money have already been spent. The planning, public hearings, condemnation, acquisition and re-location of the land and the approval of the plan at various state, local and national levels, have already taken place.

When you walk into the local agency to talk about a vacant Urban Renewal site, as many as six or seven (or even more) years have gone by before the agency feels it is ready to dispose of the land to you, the prospective developer. All of these six or seven years of motion and all of these funds have gone to waste unless you, Mr. Redeveloper, can get the project off the ground and actually build and rent it up.

The Political Considerations

Bear in mind that the last half-dozen or more years have been fraught with local political acrimony. The re-located people did not want to leave; they did not want to see their homes torn down and their businesses destroyed. Re-locating these "slum dwellers" created pressures as they moved into new neighborhoods, and many a politician lies buried in the political boneyard in his community because he said or did the wrong thing about Urban Renewal. Every added day that goes by in which the city continues to own that vacant Urban Renewal land irritates old wounds.

The people who opposed the project in the first place constantly write to the mayor, griping about the fact that their people have been dispersed, their homes gone, and that there is nothing but an eye-sore, an empty lot, strewn with rubble where their homes used to be. Homes that were blighted enough to warrant condemnation where rats once frolicked now achieve an aura of grandeur—an aura not possible before the bulldozer cleared the site. Now, all we have is an empty site with a bombed-out look that the local citizenry refers to as "Hiroshima Flats."

If only something could be built—the large marble civic center set forth in the brochure which looks so good in the architect's rendering. If only those 13,000 family units could rise on the empty site—it would all have been worth it—and the mayor could have his picture taken cutting the ribbon as the first family moves in.

You, the redeveloper, walk into the LPA and promise to do this. No wonder you are welcomed. What we have sketched above is a typical political background. If you are not welcomed when you walk in—run as if the very devil is pursuing you, because you are about to enter into a partnership with the local renewal agency and if they do not want you and do not promise to love, honor and obey you, forget it. This is not the place for you.

The LPA's

If you pick up your local telephone book you will find in almost any city in the United States an Urban Renewal or Urban Development agency. If you cannot find it in the phone book, call the mayor's office. Each year, the United States Department of Housing and Urban Development publishes an Urban Renewal Directory which lists the location, on a state-by-state and city-by-city basis, of all Urban Renewal agencies together with the projects they then have pending and the amount of dollars involved. Most of the information in this chapter comes from William Swayze, HUD's Chief Real Estate officer in the New York area.

In addition, the Renewal Assistance Administration of HUD, from time to time, publishes a list of land available for private development, broken down city by city and showing by thousands of square feet the land available for private redevelopment, sub-classified as to family, multi-family (residential), commercial, and industrial plottage and showing the Local Public Agency address which has the available land.

Greater detail, of course, may be found by visiting the Local Public Agency, but a quick glance at a recent listing supplied by William Swayze, of HUD, showed parcels as small as 10,000 feet available for commercial redevelopment in Fairbanks, Alaska, to over 1,000,000 feet in East Hartford, Connecticut, for commercial development. There were available 1-1/2 million square feet for single-family homes in Georgia, and many, many others. The Urban Renewal Directory referred to above ran over 100 pages and listed communities participating in the program ranging all the way from Alabama to Wisconsin and including Puerto Rico and the Virgin Islands.

Your First Step

In any case, if you want to get involved in the Urban Renewal program, your first step should be the Local Public Agency where you can have the local administrator outline to you briefly what he has available together with an approximate timetable as to when each of his projects will "take off." After you have picked out the area or areas most interesting to you and your organization, you should walk away with a copy of the printed Urban Renewal plan.

You should take the Plan home and read it at least two or three times—the first time superficially, to get a feeling of what is going on, and later, in greater detail. Next, you should get into your car and drive around the area selected, trying to visualize what it will look like when the overall plan is completed. You should also try to visualize what the area will look like while you try to rent it (i.e., are you going to be the first builder and are the other adjacent projects going to be completed before yours or after yours). It will make a difference in your rental timetable if the neighboring areas are cleared, rebuilt or still slums.

What is the LPA Like?

The remainder of this section will discuss what you want

from the LPA. After all, they are not only going to sell you some
land, but they are going to be your partner for a number of years
to come. So you should find out exactly what they can and cannot
do as early as possible. You must know how enthusiastic they are
about you, and determine in your own mind whether you are enthusiastic about them.

After going through some of the major problems detail by
detail, we will wind up by giving you a checklist which points up to
you some of the unique profit-making opportunities of Urban Renewal, as well as the more important traps and pitfalls.

Negotiating to Buy Urban Renewal Property— Your Contract with the LPA

Most of the problems in this section are problems that are
going to be faced by your lawyer. But you must understand them,
too, because they represent the key problems and solutions that
are part of your deal.

The typical Urban Renewal land purchase contract bears no
more resemblance to the ordinary real estate contract than 4th of
July fireworks resemble the Agena II Rocket. Unless you've been
through an Urban Renewal deal before, neither you nor your lawyer
will be prepared for some of the problems that will arise. It is
the purpose of this section of the book to outline many of those
pitfalls and to suggest to you some of the answers that have been
worked out by developers and their attorneys who have been through
deals like yours.

Many Government Agencies Control You

To begin with, no other real estate deal you have ever done
involves so many lawyers of governmental agencies—at the federal,
state and local levels. Bear in mind, however, that almost one
billion dollars worth of these projects have already been completed—
and many billions are going to be done. This should prove that
while the problems are formidable, they have been dealt with by
others and you can deal with them, too. It just takes "know-how"
and imagination.

While this section will deal with the problems from an over-all viewpoint, all real estate deals involve local law which may require modification in your particular area. On every occasion where Urban Renewal lawyers work, they always work with a local attorney as co-counsel.

Know Your LPA

Let us discuss your contract to buy part of an Urban Renewal development. The first question is "Whom do you deal with?" Your local agency will probably be called the Urban Renewal Agency, or the Housing and Redevelopment Agency, and you will probably be dealing with the Director or the Assistant Director thereof. You will find that he is going to be your best friend throughout the job. He is rooting for you—he may even encourage you when you get disgusted yourself. He will help, as best he can, to pass along to you his experience through the red tape maze of his own community.

Since you cannot do the job without his assistance, you must ask yourself at the very beginning, how competent he is. How much power has he got? If you find yourself in a situation where the Urban Renewal Director has little or no authority—where the deals are being handed out in the back room—forget it. Just leave.

There is no point in wasting your time there. You don't want to get yourself involved in a political hassle. These deals are hard enough to do if everyone is pulling together. We have run into situations where the Local Public Agency is a semi-autonomous organization largely financed with federal funds—and a law unto itself. That is fine. It enables them to hire more capable people because they're not surrounded with the usual budgetary limitations. However, if the LPA has engendered the hostility of all the people it has to deal with—bear in mind that its projects will move more slowly and be encumbered by more red tape than if there is thorough cooperation all around.

The LPA's Relationships
with Other Agencies

You will learn soon enough whether the LPA has a good relationship with the regional office of the Department of Housing and Redevelopment; with the FHA; with the City Council and the mayor's office. You will see some authorities where the director gets on the telephone and speaks to his counterparts at the other agencies, pointing out his problems and making requests and asking what can be done. In other agencies, the director throws up his hands and asks you to clear all your own paper work. It won't take you very long to find out whether you're in a mess or not.

What to Ask the LPA

Perhaps your first visit to the LPA would be to have a frank talk with the administrator and ask him what land is available and when it is going to be available. He will pull out his Urban Renewal Plan and his maps and show you that he has a piece of industrial land, and a luxury apartment house here and an office building site there, etc., etc. You will ask him (if you don't already know) at what stage those land acquisition programs are in.

In other words, is he merely in the planning stage or has he already acquired title? If he has acquired title, has he re-located the people living there, and, if he has re-located them, has he demolished?

In some cases, the land will be ready for immediate disposition. The LPA will have acquired title, re-located all of the families living on it, demolished their housing and prepared the site.

You will ask for a copy of the Urban Renewal Plan, a great, thick book which not only contains maps, but restrictions as to the various sites. It tells what the land can and cannot be used for, shows the zoning of the proposed sites, and the size and type of building you can use. There will be rights-of-way descriptions (which tell you where the new streets are going to be), what roads are going to be acquired, and what public facilities built by the city. Street improvements, sewer improvements, storm drains, water systems, electric systems, traffic control, telephone and gas systems will all be discussed and mapped.

Facts of Life on Community
Participation

For almost twenty years the decisions as to what kind of housing was best for the community were made by urban planners, Washington officials, the LPA administrator, the Chamber of Commerce, the mayor's brother-in-law, the local builder, and just about everyone except the people who were going to live there. Commencing with the 1966-1967 riots in such areas as Detroit, New Haven, Newark, and other municipalities (which felt they had leaned over backwards in dispensing largesse), everyone began to take a greater interest in "community groups" such as churches, block organizations, neighborhood associations, etc. Indeed, not only did LPA administrators in most cities begin to seek out these local groups and get their opinion, but HUD, in Washington also pledged that nothing more would be built in the urban renewal areas unless and until the community itself demonstrated that it was behind the particular project 100%.

As a result, it behooves you, on your early visits to the LPA, to find out what the status of community organizations is, whom these organizations represent, how they feel about the particular project, etc. If your' job is going to have to be "cleared with Sidney," it is most important to find out who "Sidney" is, whom he represents, and how he feels about your particular job.

Timetables

You will ask the administrator for a realistic timetable on when the land will be available for you. He may not stick to it, but you can be sure that if he tells you he is three or four years away from being able to dispose of the property (because he still has re-location problems on his hands) you can be sure that the property is not going to be available any sooner.

You will want to ask him about some of the things that you may not find in the Urban Renewal Plan. Among the important advantages which cannot be found in most Urban Renewal plans is the ability to get some kind of tax reduction or abatement. Since real estate taxes may run 25% or 30% of the cost of operating a residential property, the desirability of the site and your ability to rent apartments on it may be governed by the kind of tax assessments you are going to get.

Real Estate Tax Concessions

Substantial tax reduction can give you a favorable rental advantage or a favorable profit margin. Real estate taxes play an even more important part in the cost of a retail or industrial development. Since real estate taxes go on and on, you may be better off building your project in an Urban Renewal area which offers tax abatement than in a neighboring project which offers no such abatement, even though the land costs may be lower. A bargain land price is no bargain if you're going to get clobbered with real estate taxes once your building is up.

Of course, we do not have to warn professionals that the informal promise of the mayor about a low assessment is meaningless, unless it can be put into some kind of contract. Mayors have been known to lose elections and to go back on their words. In many states, cities and counties, such tax abatement is not legal. In other areas, tax reduction depends on a local law, and your lawyer will have to look it up to make sure what your rights will be.

Limited Dividends and Other Controls

In some cases, only so long as the builder accepts some part of a limited dividend or modified rent control will he get tax benefits. Again, this is a matter of local law. You will generally find the LPA knows the facts—but sometimes if you don't ask for them, they may be overlooked in your calculations and you may walk away from a job that somebody else will be delighted to do.

Some states and localities have special assistance and financing programs available to help urban development. An example is New York State's Mitchell-Lama Act which offers direct loans from the State on a long-term basis at below market interest rates (a program quite similar to FHA's § 221(d)(3) program).

Local Code Compliance

You will also be looking for traps that are not apparent in the Urban Renewal Plan. If you are an out-of-town builder, you will want to take back with you a copy of the local building code and make sure what kind of restrictive fire, electrical and construction problems you may run into. In some cases the building codes may force you to walk away from an otherwise desirable job. On the other hand, in some situations you may be able to get the city to give you a variance from the building code's restrictions. In this area you will find the Urban Renewal Administrator on your side against the building department—and since he knows his way around locally, he will be your greatest friend.

Local General Contractor?

Many Urban Renewal builders prefer to do their jobs as joint ventures. Even though they may do the planning, they insist on taking in a local contractor as their partner. This has a dual advantage. The local man is respected locally, and he is able to handle some of the political problems that an out-of-towner would have. As far as the local community is concerned, the local name guarantees performance, and your local general contractor will know his way around the building codes better than you do. He will know who the appropriate local architect is, while you, as the out-of-towner, will be able to bring your own knowledge of FHA or Urban Renewal financing to bear. You may have greater resources and better financing than could be obtained locally and possibly better design specialists and more knowledgable Urban Renewal lawyers than could be found locally. These jobs are big enough so that you're better off owning one-third of three of them and doing them all rather than killing yourself on one with a half-baked team.

Amend the Urban Renewal Plan?

What do you do if you find sections of the Urban Renewal Plan that you're not happy with? Bear in mind that the printed pamphlet, although it has gone through an awful lot of work, is not necessarily the last word on the subject. The Urban Renewal Authority can—and in many instances has—amended its plan. It's important to know that many of these plans were drawn by specialists who were not fully familiar with the local situation—and if you feel the project would be better if a street opened on one side than on the other, or if the view faced one way, as distinguished from the other, you may be able to get the Plan changed. Bear in mind that the LPA is your greatest friend in these areas. They want you to have a successful project, and if they can get the Plan amended, they will.

Major or Minor Plan Change?

It is important to note that getting an Urban Renewal Plan modified can be quite a complicated procedure. The first question one runs into is: Is this a minor change or a major change in the Plan? No one can tell you whether a particular change is minor or major. You will have to consider the overall objective of the Plan. If the LPA decides it is a minor change, you will only need local city council approval and that will be the end of it. The Department of Housing and Urban Development does not ordinarily object to "minor" changes. But if the change is going to be a "major" one—and it is the regional office of HUD that decides whether it is "major" or not—then you will have to clear it with not only the LPA and all the local municipal agencies, but also the various federal agencies, with the result that you may have a six to nine month time lag. Furthermore, there will be a need for new "land use" appraisals (which may increase the land cost to you). Those new appraisals will take time, and there is no telling what they will come in at.

In spite of this, if you still feel that the Urban Renewal Plan is not suitable, you will be better off waiting to get what you want than getting involved in a difficult project. Don't be afraid to ask for changes—if you need them and if you're willing to put in the time necessary to get them.

Chapter III

MORE LAND BUYING PROBLEMS IN URBAN RENEWAL

Other Problems

In assessing the timetable, it is good to know whether all the political ferment and litigation has died down. In other words, you want to know whether the condemnation has been passed on by the courts—whether good title has been procured by the LPA—and, if so, whether you will be able to get title insurance on the land and on what terms.

Remember, you may be putting a $20 million structure on a $200,000 piece of marked-down land. While the title company may have to take a risk for the LPA on its $200,000 acquisition program, they may not be willing to issue insurance to you on $20 million worth of building if there is some kind of a title problem. Before you get through you will not only be checking and re-checking most of your paper work with your title company, but also with potential mortgage lenders. More about that later.

Extra Costs

It is wise to remember that all Urban Renewal contracts

compel you to comply with a large number of minimum wage statutes and with an equally large number of anti-discrimination statutes relating not only to hiring but to renting and selling. Your
calculations should take into consideration the cost of hiring public
relations talent, because no matter what you do in these fields,
you're bound to see some pickets before you're through.

You need to know something about the timing of the peripheral
improvements. You look at a map and you see there is going to be
a great, big, new connecting highway. But when? Are you going
to be expected to rent up and to build before it's in? Is the road
going to be in before you're started?

Co-ordination

The Urban Renewal Plan shows that your luxury apartment
house will be facing a new office building center. Are your luxury
apartments going to go up before the center is built or after it?
At present, there is a garbage dump there. Are you going to be
able to rent until the office buildings go up? What will prospective
tenants say if they face the existing garbage dump? Perhaps this
problem can be overcome by turning the buildings around so that
they face the other way. These are the kinds of things that have to
be considered.

Timing of Supporting Facilities

We have spoken about roads—but what about schools, buses,
shopping, street lighting, sewers, etc? When are they going to be
in? Your timing must tie together with the Urban Renewal authority's and your contract should cover those timing problems.

If yours is a retail or shopping center project—who is going
to supply the parking space? Are you going to open before the
city's lot is available? Obviously, you're going to need parking
space when you're ready to open. Your contract and the city's
should be tied together in some way.

Mortgages

You are, of course, going to want to know where your financing is going to come from. We deal with FHA financing in another section of this book but at this point we want to mention that if your project is conditioned upon getting some kind of FHA mortgage—your contract should mention it. You will certainly, while you are drawing up your contract, want to be checking with the FHA to find out what kind of a mortgage is available.

The problems of the early years of Urban Renewal and FHA have been overcome. In those earlier days we faced situations where the Urban Renewal administration would put one price on the land (for disposition purposes) only to find the price was unacceptable to the Federal Housing Authority for mortgage purposes. Now, co-ordination between these agencies results in both FHA and Urban Renewal agreeing on land values. You should therefore inquire from the LPA whether disposition appraisals have been made, what values have been fixed, and how these tie together with the FHA figures.

Is there any other kind of financing available? In some cities, local chambers of commerce have set up civic groups to help finance Urban Renewal projects. In some cases, local revenue bond financing is available. In other cases, local civic groups will help you with publicity and community relations. It may be important to have them pitch in, take you around the community and "sponsor you," especially if you're an out-of-towner.

Is There a Market?

Now that you've gotten most of the information together, you'll want to go to the quiet of your own office and calculate the construction cost of the project. What will the financing cost you? Where will it come from? What kind of FHA mortgage are you going to get? How long will it take to do it? Will you finance it all at once, or will you do the job in several chunks? Will it be rentable, and at what price? Is there a market at that price?

You will want to do your own market study. The new computer-type information available from such organizations as Barrett, at nominal cost, can now save you months of research in determining whether a market exists at your projected price.

If you're going to get FHA financing, you'll want to go into the FHA local office and have a pre-application conference with them to see if they agree with your analysis about economic feasibility.

Assembling the Team

At this point you will want to start assembling your team—if you haven't already done so. You will either need to hire your own people on a full-time basis, or you'll need to bring in the best outside consultants you can lay your hands on. You will certainly need a knowledgable tax consultant. You will need an accountant who must understand construction accounting and the requirements of FHA (if you're going to use FHA financing) plus a top real estate attorney, preferably one with FHA and Urban Renewal experience. You will need an architect who has had some experience in the community. Your architect must also know Urban Renewal and FHA. You will put all these fellows to work checking out your conclusions before you get ready to bid. Later, you will need to add more people to the team—public relations and advertising experts, landscape architects, and rental and management people.

Buying Your Land

You should know that most LPA's have a half dozen different ways of disposing of their land. Briefly, they are:

1. Running an auction.

2. Soliciting sealed bids and selling to the highest bidder.

3. Negotiating with a number of competitive bidders and then disposing under open conditions.

4. Public auction, with minimum upset price.

5. A fixed price, with the bidding on a competitive design or other competitive basis.

6. Negotiated sale.

7. Pre-determined price offering.

Not all of these methods are available in every state. For example, in some states the law requires either sealed bids or public auction.

Ten years of experience have made LPA's veer away from straight auction-type building. They discovered that the highest bidder was not always the most capable developer. In fact, if you think about it, with all of the problems in Urban Renewal, the highest bidder is most likely an inexperienced amateur.

Design Competitions

Another method of disposing of land has fallen by the wayside, as a result of ten years of experience. It is the "design competition." While I am sure there are some LPA's still using it, most LPA administrators have abandoned the design competition. The design competition asked builders to propose the best plan for the land. The builders were told that the price for the land was fixed, but that the builder making the best presentation would win the project.

A large, prestigious architectural board was established and developers came from all over the country and spent sums ranging up to six figures. Each prepared newer and more dramatic presentations. Responsible developers soon learned to stay away from these design competitions like from the plague. You may spend $50,000 or $100,000 and then find you have a set of worthless plans on your hands because the panel picked someone else.

The Price is "Too Good"

Similarly, ten years of experience has shown LPA that getting the maximum price for the land only forces builders to squeeze on the construction end of the budget or to increase tenant rentals. In some instances, overpaying for the land results in a project's failure. The LPA really wants a finished project of optimum value to the community, built as quickly as possible (so as to return it to the tax rolls). Getting the best land price means little, especially since five-sixths of the money may be state or federal funds.

Sometimes, special consideration is given to retail store tenants, owner-users, or other occupants who formerly occupied part of the Urban Renewal area. They are given preferences in re-locating within the project area or in an adjacent project area. The Urban Renewal manual recognizes such preferences and in quite a number of instances groups of local retailers have banded together to develop a section to re-locate themselves in new stores, within the renewal area.

Sponsors

Generally, the best position for a developer to have in those situations where the LPA permits it, is to be a "sponsor." In the gobbledygook of the Urban Renewal manual, the sponsor is permitted to "negotiate disposal under other than open competitive conditions." This does not mean that you can make a secret deal. Your deal must be open to the public—but the Urban Renewal agency can prefer you over competition and make any deal with you it wants, provided it gets the appraised re-use value for the land. Generally, the sponsor gets the "inside track." In other words, if you sit down with LPA early enough and if they consider you a desirable prospect, they will spend time with you, perhaps make changes in the plan with you, make an effort to cut out the parcel you want, and enter into a mutually satisfactory contract.

Tips and Warnings for Sponsors

It is important not to go overboard on design costs, money commitments, etc., until a final, formal contract is signed. Many sponsors have spent time and money only to find that the LPA has changed its mind and selected another sponsor, or someone with a different design. Bear in mind that until you have a signed contract with the LPA, all you have is "the inside track." That track may lead nowhere.

The LPA will ordinarily seek to honor its moral obligations, since it cannot build up relations with builders if it's going to "welsh" on its deals. The advantage of the sponsorship technique is that the builder gets a chance to work things out informally with the LPA before going to contract. Thus, you may ask for modifications and submit a number of informal sketches to get the LPA's reactions, without spending the kind of money that's involved in a formalized "design." Usually, these informal sponsorship agreements build a relationship between the developer and the LPA. An understanding of each other's strengths and weaknesses develops out of the many negotiations that take place and, hopefully, a flexible arrangement is worked out so that formal land disposition contracts can be signed. An outsider finds it hard to compete with the sponsor because he hasn't put in the same number of hours studying the project, nor has he developed the same relationship with the LPA.

Open Competitive Disposition

The sponsorship technique involved arms-length negotiations between the LPA and the sponsor. Another common method of disposition is to negotiate sale under "open competitive disposition." Negotiated dispositions and open competitive conditions generally involve an advertisement by the LPA requesting the public to submit proposals. A date is fixed as the last day on which proposals will be accepted. Then the LPA goes through all the documents evaluating such factors as the amount of time the builder believes it will take him to complete the project, the price offered for the property, the benefit to the community in terms of sociological, financial and architectural values. These, plus the financial ability of the builder and his qualifications, are used to select the "winner." This technique differs from sponsorship in that the LPA is considering a number of submissions at the same time without offering the negotiating flexibility of the sponsorship technique.

The criticism offered is that "open competition" lacks flexibility and offers less opportunity to the builder to use his know-how. The advantage of this technique (as distinguished from sponsorship) is that it offers less opportunity for chicanery—or for charges of chicanery. This "open competition" technique was far commoner in the early stages of Urban Renewal when most LPA administrators were afraid they would expose themselves to criticism if they dealt only with one possible developer on a particular site. However, with experience has come sophistication and courage, so that as land inventories have piled up, many more LPA's have taken to direct negotiations and "sponsorship."

Examining the Plan

What kind of documents and information will you need, as you and your attorney begin to go over a proposed contract with the LPA? Certainly, you will want to look at the disposition very carefully to decide on the amount of acreage you are going to get. You will want to check out your zoning and discover the proposed minimum price for the parcel. Your price is based, usually, on the "re-use appraisals" which the LPA has acquired. Some LPA's will show you their appraisals, or at least discuss them with you frankly, while others keep them under their hat. In any event, you will certainly need to know the price of the land you propose to buy (although, sometimes if the surveys have not been completed your price will be expressed as a "price per square foot").

Unusual Title Problems

The LPA's form of contract will usually mention in it the form of deed which you will get when title passes. This may vary anywhere from a quit claim deed to a warranty deed, depending on local practice. The deed will contain clauses calculated to scare the usual real estate lawyer to death, if he has never been through an Urban Renewal project before. What is worse, the clauses in the deed will not only frighten the title lawyer, but also the conventional mortgage lender's attorney, unless he has been through an Urban Renewal project before.

For example, the deed will usually contain such clauses as a right to re-enter the land and even forfeiture with reversion of title to the LPA in the event the covenants of the deed are breached. Outside of the Urban Renewal area you will rarely see a deed that provides for a forfeiture—and the usual mortgage lender will ordinarily never lend on such a deed. However, lenders who have dealt with Urban Renewal before are familiar with the problems and even new lenders can learn from past successes.

Safeguards

Sometimes to be found in the land contract or deed, and sometimes merely incorporated by reference to the redevelopment plan itself, are detailed descriptions of the project area, restrictions as to use, density, building heights and areas. Also to be found in the deed or contract will be the restrictions, reservations, easements, liens, covenants, charges and benefits which the LPA needs so that it may safeguard its rights to enforce the redevelopment plan. Rights of enforcement for breaches of the redevelopment plan to the LPA and to other governmental bodies may also be found. All the documents must be read carefully with a view toward financing, re-sale and possible litigation.

Overcoming the Problems

If you go over these problems carefully, most of them can be overcome. It is only in a case where LPA is unsophisticated that you have any real trouble in this area.

You will also discover that LPA lawyers (like lawyers in general) come in three kinds—good, bad and indifferent. The good ones are a joy to work with; they will often have a greater knowledge of the intricacies of Urban Renewal projects than your own lawyer. This is particularly true if LPA counsel has had a number of years of experience in an active LPA. On the other hand, many LPA attorneys receive their training in other civil service positions, and many lack a strong background in real estate and title law. If they are open-minded and intelligent about it, you will be able to get most of the modifications you need to finance and build your deal.

If you are dealing with incompetent counsel at the LPA, your life will be a horror. You may have to walk away from the job as early as possible and come back a couple of years later—by which time you will find that the pressure of failure in other jobs may have forced the LPA to replace him.

Other Available Data

Among the other documents the LPA may have available and which you should ask for are test borings, market analysis and re-use appraisals. These re-use appraisals are required of the LPA by HUD, but there is nothing that compels the LPA to show them to you.

However, many experienced LPA's will be glad to show them to you. Then, if the appraisers have gone off half-cocked, you will point out the factual information to the LPA and they may be able to get new appraisals. This helps get the land marked down to a realistic basis. You will certainly—if you're going to use FHA financing—want to make certain that both the LPA and the FHA are in agreement as to the re-use value.

Overcoming Restrictions

When you get your set of documents and begin to examine them, you or your attorney may come across a number of restrictions that make building or financing quite difficult. If that be the case, particularly if you are dealing with a negotiated deal, you will want to call the LPA's attention thereto and, hopefully, get changes. In some cases, the height and use restrictions will be

38

unrealistic; in other cases, the restrictions will prevent your bringing in the amenities necessary to sell or rent the project. In one reported case, the Urban Renewal plan provided that all plans should pass an architectural board of review. Unfortunately, the architectural reviewer "hated" multi-family housing—the only kind that could be built on the site.

Financing and Restrictions

Not only will you and your attorney want to look at all these documents—but again, if you're going to use non-FHA conventional financing, you might start your lender looking at them as early as possible.

Your Architect

Also, your architect should get into the act as early as possible. He will want to read the restrictions, look up the building codes, and see whether your project is buildable, from an architectural viewpoint. Furthermore, you will probably want to check the documents out with the potential lender's title company. You are certainly going to need mortgage title insurance, because neither FHA nor any conventional lender will permit a loan without the standard American title-form of insurance.

Soil Conditions

In examining the various documents submitted by the LPA and in getting ready to sign a contract, you had better make certain what condition the land will be in, on delivery. This does not only mean the usual borings and testings, but also the condition it will be in when you get it. In other words, is the LPA going to give you a nicely bulldozed and compacted site, or is it going to give you a pile of rubble? Or, are you going to get a site with the old buildings still standing on it, and must you do the demolition? Whatever the facts are, they affect the overall price of the land and the amount of cash you are going to have to put into the job.

Utilities—Sewers—Roads

Also, there are timing and costs to installing such utilities as water, gas, sewer, electric, telephone and power lines. You may feel that this is the city's problem, but it may turn out to be your problem if you are going to develop "jumbo blocks" in which the streets may belong to you. It is vital that you find out as early as possible who's going to do all the off-site improvement work. If you are going to do it, you must ask yourself how you are going to finance it and whether the FHA will allow it under the mortgage.

As mentioned above, it is most important to know the timing, also. Not only must you know it, but you have to get contractual rights controlling that timing. You're not going to be able to rent your project if the streets are not in; and you're not going to be able to get them in on time to rent your project unless you have some way of forcing somebody to put them in.

Your Rights Against the LPA

Always remember, in dealing with the LPA, that it doesn't do any good to get a contract drawn "your way" unless the LPA has the authority and the funds to do the required work. You're not interested in a suit for breach of contract after you've got $7 million wrapped up in a job. You want the required work done. If the LPA has promised things it cannot deliver, you are in trouble. A lawsuit will not solve the problem.

We mentioned before that you should do your own test borings. In one situation, we discovered that an LPA site offered to our client ran down an old canal bed. In other cases, old housing that had been on the site was able to make do, even though located in an old swamp. However, such land could not support a modern office building without expensive piling. Do not rely on the LPA's borings without doing your own.

Redeveloper's Statement

When you become seriously interested in the project and ask that a contract be submitted for signature, you will be required by the LPA to submit two forms which have been set up by the HUD: Form 6004—Part I and Part II. These are called "Redeveloper's

Statement of Public Disclosure," and "Redeveloper's Statement of Qualifications and Financial Responsibility."

The first form is a public disclosure of the terms of the deal. The second form is used by the LPA and HUD to evaluate your financial ability to complete the project. The second form is kept confidential, since it entails personal financial information. The first form generally outlines the nature of your project, who you are, and what the price is going to be. The "Disclosure Form" is, of course, going to be made public. When you are given these forms, you must decide the name and form of the entity which is going to take title for you and sign the contract. You also need a rough idea of how you are going to finance the project, because the form asks these questions. You will need a preliminary idea of your planned equity money and where the equity is going to come from.

Your Deposit or Bond

Now, let's assume that all has gone well and that you and the LPA are on contract terms—that you've done your preliminary homework and are satisfied with the job. How much money are you going to have to put up, and when? Usually, the LPA will ask you to make a deposit, at the time you sign your contract to buy the land—that deposit will run from 5% to 10% of the amount bid. In many cases, you will be able to convince the LPA to accept surety bond instead of taking cash. If you have a good credit line, paying the premium on the bond may be cheaper than tying up the working capital. Of course, you may be able to get the LPA to cut the deposit (to the 5% minimum required by HUD) if you are able to show them how much money you have already spent on architectural work, market surveys, etc. You may be able to get "credit" for these expenditures one way or the other.

Who Shall Take Title?

In selecting the entity which is to be the contracting party, you will consider the financial ability and responsibility of the entity whose credit you are putting on the line. You will also take tax considerations into mind. In other words, you must decide whether to use a partnership, a corporation, a real estate trust, etc. If you are an out-of-city corporation, you may consider a joint venture with a local contractor and you may want to use a name in which there is local pride rather than your out-of-town name. Your "name" can be important for public relations and politically. It is just as absurd for the Peoria Acres Realty Corp. to plan a job in a New York City slum clearance project, as vice versa.

The Road Map—Step by Step

Since we keep stressing the subject of timing, let us step back from techniques of negotiating to view the timing problem. Suppose you have come to a face-to-face, hand-shake understanding with the LPA. What happens next?

Well, first you'll be asked to submit your proposition by way of a letter or other document, which is merely "an invitation to enter into a contract" together with the two forms of Redeveloper's Statement H6004 discussed above. Several drafts of the formal contract will be prepared until one is finally agreed on. Then the contract is sent along to the regional office of HUD for approval before signing. It may kick around at HUD for a while. There can be some inter-office correspondence between HUD and LPA—probably with your pitching in—and then the document is ready for signatures. However, if it has been floating back and forth between agencies long enough, you may want to revise the timetable set forth in the agreement. Something may have come up in the meantime and you may ask for a modification. You may discover that the modification you are suggesting (since it calls for a "use" change) may be considered by HUD as a "major" plan change. If that is so, you may have to start running the gauntlet all over again.

What should you be doing between the time you have your handshake with the LPA and the time you finally sign your contract? The conservative and cautious thing to do would be to do nothing. In that way you will not be incurring any expenses until you know you have a binding deal. But, let's look at the other possibilities.

What to Do While You Wait?

If you take the conservative, cautious viewpoint and wait, you may never get anything done. You may decide to take a calculated risk (most developers do) and move your job along while you wait, drawing plans, taking test borings, fishing around for financing, getting estimates, etc. In many cases you may even have a signed contract but not yet have received the delivery of title (because some work has to be done first by the LPA or for some other reason). Possibly, re-location may still be going on, on part of the site; or maybe demolition is still taking place.

If you have a signed contract, it is possible to do construction work on your site prior to delivery of title. If your timing is right, you might want to do that. The problem, of course, is how to finance this kind of construction work prior to passage of title. You will have great difficulty in getting construction lending until you do take title. Nevertheless, you may decide to do some work between contract and closing of title—especially work which may hold up the job later. Some work must be done before the ground gets frozen, before the streets are in, etc.

The License to Enter the Land

Generally, this pre-title work will be done by an agreement between you and the LPA. The form of the agreement is usually checked by HUD. It is a form of license which permits you to enter onto the land before title passes. I know of at least one case where the redeveloper with a tight timetable discovered that it would take a fair amount of time to get a license agreement cleared by both LPA and HUD, so he decided to go ahead without a license. He spoke to the LPA administrator informally and then just sent some bulldozers in and did the demolition without getting a license. Of course, had there been any fuss about it, the buildings would have been gone and the LPA would have been in a position to say that permission had never been granted—so its skirts were clean. It would have been difficult for the LPA to demonstrate any damage; so it would seem that no one had been hurt by the illegal actions of the developer in entering on the land too soon. But, that is strong medicine. You will usually want written permission to start early.

Time to Perform

Other timing problems involve the time for your performance. Suppose you commit yourself to submit plans by a certain date, start construction by a certain date and finish construction by another date.

What happens if your plans are acceptable to LPA but not to the FHA? Suppose the plans are accepted by the FHA—but only after seven or eight months of horsing around? Suppose the financing is not available when you expect it, but will be later on? Suppose FHA issues its commitment, but the lending institution has trouble getting the money together in a tight money market? Any of these problems may throw your timing off. You must provide for extensions in your contract.

Piecemeal Performance

Should you break your job into separate parcels? Won't you prefer to build the apartment house first, the office building second, and the motel last—instead of all three together? If so, you will need a separate description, a separate commitment, and a separate contract as to each parcel so that they can be separated for financing and title reasons. You may have a battle with the LPA on this. They may want the whole thing packaged together. What happens if you build a perfectly valid apartment house and never get the other two projects off the ground? What protection will you have, and what protection will your mortgage lenders have? Surely, you are not both to be deemed in default, nor your equities wiped out, because of something beyond your control?

What if it was in your control and you were unable to perform? Generally speaking, you will find that the FHA will want separate parcels and separate commitments to prevent this kind of problem from arising—so you'll be able to get them on your side, in bargaining with the LPA—if you're dealing with an FHA commitment.

Excuses for Non-Performance

Again, some of your timing will depend on the speed with which third parties (including the LPA and the city) act. For example, how are you going to hook up your sewer lines until the LPA or the city has supplied the trunks? Also, how will you rent your apartments and get them ready for occupancy until the utilities are in? Also, it is good to know about the LPA's authority and the city's financial ability to perform their chores.

For example, suppose the LPA has committed itself to do something—but the federal government holds up the funds reimbursing the LPA for an earlier grant—so the LPA cannot get the money to you. What do you do then? Some of these problems can be solved by your lawyer in drawing the contract; others are business risks, pure and simple. If you must sue, it is costly and will affect your ability to get other jobs from the community, and it may affect the rest of your relationship with the LPA which may have quite a number of years to go. Remember, the LPA is your partner, and you don't sue your partner while there is any life left in the partnership.

Buying Versus Renting

Quite a number of these problems can be avoided if you are able to lease the land rather than to buy it. When you are a tenant rather than an owner, your title money cannot be spent by the LPA, and since you look forward to a long term of future rent payments, you may be able to offset any delay or damages against those rental payments. You may even be able to get the rent payments to start later. True, a lease has problems of its own, but, if timing problems are going to be serious ones, you might decide to lease your land instead of buying it. There is more discussion about leasing later on.

Comparing the Lease with a Purchase

In deciding to lease, you should find out whether the annual rental payments will exceed the cost of mortgage debt service or vice versa. Of course, under the lease you will not have to put any money into buying land. Under the mortgage you will have to spend a sum ranging from 3% to 10% of the equity to buy it (the rent will come from the mortgage).

Leasehold Carrying Charges

In many cases, land costs in Urban Renewal projects are so low in relation to the total job, that a 3% to 10% equity in the land will not be the major consideration in deciding on a lease as against a purchase.

Sometimes, what looks like a small edge in favor of leasing will be offset by the additional complexity of the leasing transaction, the greater difficulty in clearing the paper work through the many levels of governmental agencies, and the smaller mortgage commitment available on leased property. In the days when leases could be obtained for as little as 4% to 5% of the land value, leasing had an advantage over even FHA financing where the annual debt costs ran from 6-3/4% to 7-1/4% (including amortization). However, during 1965-66 when the governmental bond market was very tight and leasing costs ran above 6%, the lease's financial advantage over the mortgage became paper-thin, and leasing's small advantage was offset by the cost of the additional paper work involved.

Covenants Running with the Land

Back again to the model form of contract for land disposition which HUD has suggested in its Urban Renewal manual. You must examine carefully the clauses which the LPA calls "covenants running with the land." The first question is: Who will be empowered to enforce these agreements? Will it be just the LPA, or is it going to be the total community? Will it be the city government or can you be sued by any disgruntled neighbor or even a competing developer?

If all those people are going to have rights to enforce the covenants, who will have rights to release you from them at a later date when their terms have expired? It is most important to designate the person or persons who will have the right to release you, if you are ever going to be able to free your land from those covenants—even 50 or 75 years from now when the need for them has long since disappeared. By that time, the LPA itself may be out of existence.

Fulfillment of Conditions

Of course, your attorney will attempt to limit the covenants running with the land to the minimum. Even where he must agree to covenants running with the land, he will try to get them automatically discharged when the LPA issues a certificate of compliance at the time the job is finished. This will be possible in some instances (not in others) depending not only on city policy, but on the nature of the covenants.

Every once in a while an overzealous LPA attorney attempts to put into the contract certain covenants, which will run with the land, that are patently absurd. Thus, one incident has been reported where the bias of one local attorney against signs with flashing lights resulted in his attempting to get a perpetual covenant running with the land against them.

No Unnecessary Burdens

It is wise to point out to the LPA that the Urban Renewal manual codifies HUD's policy on the subject of land restrictions. The manual says that the agreement should be drafted to safeguard the interests of the project "without burdening the developer with unnecessary risk or obligations that may impair the marketability or value of the land or the ability of the redeveloper to obtain financing." In instances where you feel the covenants are obviously absurd, you may be able to consult with title authorities and come to the conclusion that they might be held invalid as unreasonable restraints on alienation. However, no one wants to go to the heartache of litigation and there can be no question that unreasonable restrictions written into your deed will affect financing ability. It is usually easier to try to knock them out right in the contract than to suffer with them afterwards.

LPA's Duties

If, on examination of your contract and the Urban Renewal program, you notice that you are permitted special zoning or other relief from the usual municipal laws, you should get a clause in your contract to the effect that the LPA will do whatever is necessary to get you the required relief. You do not want to get in the middle of a hassle with the building department when you try to get your building permits and are ready to start collecting rents.

Anti-Speculation Provisions

There are quite a number of clauses in the standard LPA agreement prohibiting you from re-selling the property at a profit until you have completed the project. These are called anti-speculation clauses, and the first reaction that your attorney will have will be to ask the LPA to take them out. LPA will not take them out. Indeed, they cannot, under the terms of their contract with the federal government. The program is planned to prevent people from entering into contracts with LPA's without the intention of building, but merely to speculate in the land.

However, bearing in mind that you're going to have to live with these anti-speculation provisions, you should at least make an effort to have the restrictions required by the LPA reasonable ones, without overburdening you. Since most of these anti-speculation clauses terminate when the project is completed, you will want a pretty careful definition of what constitutes completion, who will determine that it has taken place, and what the standards for that determination shall be. Will the issuance of a certificate of occupancy be enough? If not, can you make it enough by contract?

If you intend to sell off a portion of the land to a co-operative apartment project, as under § 213, or to a condominium, as under § 234, obviously you are going to need to sell part of the land. Your whole plan in developing the rest of the sites may depend on your making a profit on that sale. Your LPA contract must, of course, cover that kind of situation.

Similarly, if you are going to do some shopping center development, retail store development, or industrial development, you may find that some of your major tenants will come in only if they can own their property. In many cases they will want a sale-leaseback, but they will insist on ownership either because of the residual benefits or because better financing can be obtained that way, with lower rental costs to the tenant. In either event, it would be wise, if you're going to handle non-residential property, if you would get—right in your contract—the power to sell certain parcels or a certain percentage of your parcels. HUD's latest anti-speculation regulations together with the LPA's past practices should be carefully examined in planning financing and drawing your contract.

Some Required Exceptions

In some cases, the anti-speculation clauses will go so far as to prohibit sales of the stock of the redeveloper without approval of the LPA. You would certainly want an exception to permit transfers of the stock within your own family, as long as certain of the officers stay with the venture. In other cases you will need rights to transfer stock to outsiders (up to a certain percentage) provided certain of the key redevelopers stay in as an aid to bringing in outside investors.

Project Commencement Date

The date by which the redeveloper should commence construction involves one of the stickiest parts of your negotiations. Ideally, you as a redeveloper, would like to see every single piece of urban land around you redeveloped, in the form of a beautiful park with all the old slums removed, before you are asked to start any work. Also, you would like to be certain that every one of the roads leading to your area—including those to be financed with federal funds—are completed.

Furthermore, you would want to make sure that the money market and the rental market are right before you start your job. Certainly, you will want to make sure that your FHA commitment (or your conventional commitment) has come in just right.

Of course, if you could get a contract like that, it would be great. Unfortunately, the LPA finds that every redeveloper wants the same clauses in his contract and that if everyone is going to wait for everyone else, nothing will ever happen. Also, the land is off the tax rolls while everyone is waiting. Lastly, while all wait, the former residents who have been re-located organize themselves into political action groups and picket LPA with signs reading "you took away our homes—now what are you doing for us?"

Obviously, your contract is going to have to balance your problems with the LPA's problems, and we have discussed both problems so that you can have a mutual feel of each other's difficulties and requirements.

How Much Down?

Another common negotiating problem involves the re-developer's deposit. First, it is important to note that there are two different kinds of deposits. In some cases a deposit is asked as an evidence of good faith when negotiations are begun, and before a contract is signed. In other cases, a second deposit is asked (or the first deposit may be applied on account of the second) at contract signing time.

The Urban Renewal manual suggests that the redeveloper's performance may be secured either by a cash deposit or by a surety company's performance bond. Wherever possible, we would prefer use of a bond because it ties up less cash. If the applicant is financially well rated, the bonding premium may be much less than the cost of idling working capital.

Cash Versus Bonds

If you're going to do an FHA project, the FHA is going to want a performance bond—and in some cases you may be able to get the LPA to consent to an endorsement on the FHA's bond. In other instances, especially where cash is tight, negotiable securities may be deposited instead of putting up cash. Finally, some redevelopers have been successful in getting the LPA to consider the large architectural and engineering costs expended by the redeveloper up to the time of the signing of contract as evidence of good faith and to accept these in reduction of the "good faith" deposit. The effect of such a clause is to put your money to work twice.

Terms of Bond

If you're going to use a surety performance bond, you will want to be absolutely certain that the language you are putting in your contract is the kind of language that would be acceptable to a bonding company. Your attorney will check the language with one or more bonding companies in advance to make sure that they will issue a bond conforming with the required language and, further, to make sure that there is some way of terminating the bond relationship when the job is completed, so that the bonding company premiums will stop and the bonding company will return your collateral to you, if any was required.

Release clauses should be put into the contract excusing default under the bond and returning any deposits thereunder, in the event of default on the part of the LPA, the FHA, or third parties.

Off-Site Improvements

In dealing with the subject of off-site preparation, it is wise, if you're going to use FHA financing, to consider carefully whether the site preparation you're going to have to do is going to be mortgageable under FHA. A typical example of this is the responsibility for street plantings and such items as underground sprinklers and lawn expenditures. Many of these items may be considered by the FHA as non-mortgageable so that it would be a big help to the redeveloper if the city would prepare these items for him and reflect it in the land price (which is mortgageable).

It is important for you to examine the contracts of adjacent developers to see if their timing coordinates with yours and also to make certain that such items as grading and road building are coordinated, so that streets meet and sidewalks connect.

Recordable Proof of Performance

It is most important that provision be made for you to get a recordable certificate, showing completion upon the happening of some automatic event such as the issuance of a certificate of occupancy, or the FHA closing, so that no one can question the validity of your conditional title thereafter, and so that your relationship with the LPA will be automatically terminated when the job is finished.

Returning once again to the anti-speculation provisions, it is important to think through in advance whether you're going to want to transfer the contract to a limited partnership or real estate investment trust, for tax reasons. If you're going to do either of those things, they should be specifically provided for.

What Does Your Lender Say?

If you are going to do FHA or conventional financing, it is well to check out your contract with the appropriate lending or insuring office before signing it, to make certain that the language has been made acceptable to them. You don't want to find out that one of the clauses in the deed is unacceptable when you come to take down your first mortgage advance.

If your project is going to get conventional financing—or if you're going to do a commercial or industrial development—you must make certain that your contract clauses are the kind that will be recognized by long-term tenants and conventional lenders.

The language of the urban redevelopment plan must be read very carefully (and probably broadened substantially) if you are going to sign long-term shopping center leases.

Since most shopping center and industrial leases involve substantial long-term financial commitments, the tenants who sign those leases want flexibility sufficient to protect themselves in the case of marketing or neighborhood changes. Thus, what was planned as a 1966 neighborhood convenience store, such as a grocery store, etc., may find itself a desirable gas station location but an impossible grocery location 20 years from now. Some kind of reasonable use modification in the future must be required and if there are covenants running with the land, they may have to be modified. You are better off insisting on getting these modifications worked out now even if they are deemed major changes in the Urban Renewal plan, than to guess about the future.

If you don't get the changes you need, you may find yourself with an unfinanceable, unrentable venture. Think these problems through with your lawyer and with your banker now—before signing—and all will be smooth later.

Checklist

Because the last two chapters cover so much and are so important, we have set up the meat of them in checklist form on the following pages to help guide you through your LPA negotiations. They are a starting point. You will want to cover many more, after going over the problems of your particular job with your lawyer.

CHECKLIST ON BUYING URBAN RENEWAL LAND

1. Visit the LPA—What to ask:
   (a) Talk to the Director; see what is available.
   (b) When will it be available?
   (c) When will the surrounding Urban Renewal projects be done?
   (d) When will the supporting roads, schools and utilities be in?
   (e) What kind of people are you dealing with? Competent? Honest? Cooperative? Political?

(f) What is the LPA's relationship with local, state and federal agencies?

(g) Get several copies of the specific Urban Renewal plan and all the amendments to date.

2. Review the Urban Renewal Plan:

(a) Give copies of the Plan to your lawyer, architect, mortgage banker and discuss their roles therin.

(b) Analyze amount of land; price per unit; land restrictions; uses; density; building codes; and esthetic controls.

(c) Who will put in (at whose expense and with what mortgageability) the roads, sewers, utilities, traffic controls?

(d) What will the surrounding neighborhood be like when you begin your renting program?

(e) Get realistic timetables (and check them out with other people) as to acquisition of site by LPA; re-location; demolition; disposition; and completion of supporting facilities.

3. Ask for the items not on the Plan:

(a) Tax rates.

(b) Local financing.

(c) Will the LPA build any of the supporting facilities? It can borrow at a lower, tax-exempt rate than you can.

(d) Site preparation and clearance? Who will do it and what will it cost?

(e) Will building and zoning codes be modified for you? If not, what effect will they have on your deal?

(f) Are you giving thought about the need to amend the Plan? If so, will it be a major or a minor plan change?

(g) Significance of major or minor plan changes (risks and advantages both ways).

(h) Some lender and title problems:
Have all court proceedings ended?
Has LPA got good insurable title?
Will you be able to get title insurance and at what cost?
Will you be able to get mortgage insurance on the structure? Land insurance is not enough. The structure is going to cost ten times the land.

4. What extra costs are built into the job?

   (a) Prevailing wages.
   (b) Anti-discrimination statutes.
   (c) Public relations costs.
   (d) Extra legal costs.
   (e) Extra paper work, red tape and delays, delays and
       more delays.
   (f) How long has it taken your competitors to get out of
       the woods in the same locality?
   (g) What effect on your renting will the peripheral area
       have? When will the peripheral construction
       work be ready?
   (h) Will you be the "last" developer or are you going to
       be the first? Your rental timetable will be
       affected.
   (i) Are you getting a sufficient discount for the delays?
   (j) Will you be able to coordinate your work with the
       neighboring work? Is the sewer contractor, the
       paving man, the public utility, etc., working with
       you or against you? Can your own men bid that
       work?

5. Financing—Which will it be—FHA, Mitchell-Lama or
   Conventional?

   (a) Leasing vs. purchasing.
   (b) Construction loan—How long? And at what interest
       rate?
   (c) Is the cost of paying construction interest going to be
       considered a mortgageable part of the job on the
       permanent financing? What happens if it runs
       longer?
   (d) See separate checklist contrasting various financing
       programs at end of chapter on FHA programs.

6. Is there a market?

   (a) Will the project rent or sell?
   (b) What is the competition like?
   (c) Have market studies been performed? By whom?
       Are they reliable? Look at the studies anyhow,
       even if you don't agree you may get some ideas.
   (d) A wealth of material should have been assembled
       which may give your people leads and raise some

questions. It also may be out of date.

(e) Will the government guaranteed loans be sufficient?
What kind of equity money is going to be
required? Where will it come from? What
must you pay for it?

7. How to negotiate your deal with the LPA:

(a) Auction.
(b) Highest sealed bid.
(c) Fixed price, but design competition.
(d) Negotiated sale (sponsor with published public
disclosure)
(e) WARNING—try to keep your investment at a minimum until your contract is signed, and title
has closed.
(f) You must do some work on speculation. Most LPA's
will take their moral obligations to you seriously.
(g) Ask to see the disposition appraisals; the condemnation appraisals; the market data; the test borings.
(h) Re-read the Urban Renewal Plan as a legal document.
Bear in mind that it will bind you for forty or
more years.
(i) Shall you propose modifications to the Plan? To the
contract? Now or later? The calculated risk
involved in delay.
(j) Calm down your attorney and your lender (if they
have never seen an LPA contract before).
Remember—others have done it. Have your
attorney educate the lender and talk to the title
insurance companies.
(k) Understand and face up to the reverter and anti-speculation provisions of the contract.
(l) Who will be able to release you from the conditions?
When? Who will be able to modify them?
Remember—they are going to ride with the land
a long time.
(m) What kind of esthetic considerations are going to be
written into your contract? Bear in mind that
there are no objective tests to get you off the
hook, if you are dealing with an opinionated
Board.

8. Coordination of your legal, architectural and contracting teams:

    (a) All these people should be working at the same time, moving the job along: your lawyer, lender; title company; architect; general contractor; LPA; local building department; and HUD. If everybody is waiting for the next piece of paper, you will never move along. All must work simultaneously.

9. Site Preparation—Who Will Do It? When? And is it mortgageable?

    (a) Bulldozed and compacted? Ready for construction, or a pile of rubble, expensive to remove?
    (b) What will it cost?
    (c) How will the cost affect your land cost?
    (d) Will the cost be recoverable in your mortgage?
    (e) Who will pay for and finance utilities, sewers, roads, landscaping, neighborhood amenities, schools, super-blocks, etc?

10. Negotiating your contract: Timing—Enforcement—Special Clauses:

    (a) What timetable are you being held to?
    (b) What "out" have you got, if one of the governmental agencies drags its feet?
    (c) Who do you collect from if there is a breach of contract?
    (d) In what name will you take title? (There are tax decisions, credit line decisions, public relations decisions—all hinging on this question).
    (e) When will you sign contract?
    (f) When will contract be approved?
    (g) How much will you have to put down as a deposit?
    (h) Can you put down a surety bond instead?
    (i) When will you take title?
    (j) When will you start paying taxes?
    (k) Can you sign contract now and take title when the surrounding neighborhood has been cleared up?
    (l) Need you take title at all?
    (m) Shall you lease instead of buy?
    (n) Can you enter into a management contract, with an option to buy?

(o) What other ways are there to tie the job down, with as little cash as possible?

(p) Will you be receiving credit for your developmental, planning and promotional costs?

(q) Shall you drag your feet until title passes, or shall you start processing right away? If you drag your feet you will cut down the amount of your cash involvement—but the amount of time lost will be immeasurable.

(r) For example, while negotiations, offers, contracts, architectural plans, financing and lawyering are going on, will you be ordering borings, estimates, plan changes, financial shopping and processing of changes at HUD?

(s) Do you want a license to get into work early, before title passes? Are you evaluating the risks that title may not pass? Shall you enter and begin site preparation even without a license? Are you evaluating the risks there?

11. Some timing problems:

(a) Beware of timing which calls for performance by a specific date. Timing should depend upon specific events, if possible. In other words, instead of committing yourself to start by a date certain, should you not commit yourself to start within 20 days of receiving an FHA commitment, etc. ?

(b) What if the building department, FHA, lender, HUD, supplier, act of God, etc. hold you up? Will you be in default? There should be no default as long as you are making bona fide efforts to procure performance. There are just too many factors outside of your control.

12. Leasing vs. buying:

(a) 8% vs. 4%, 5%, 6% or 7%. Which costs less, leasing or buying?

(b) Lease with option to buy.

(c) The small deal.

(d) What effect will the anti-speculation provisions have on your getting financing? Are you going to be compelled to sell part of the land as part of the deal. Get release clauses now.

(e) Contrast the effect of leasing vs. buying.

13. <u>Special problems with architect's contract:</u>

   (a) Variation from standard A. I. A. forms.

   (b) Variation from standard payments schedule, to meet FHA requirements.

   (c) Special requirements that architects meet—FHA, M. P. S. He must be an <u>independent</u> architect.

   (d) Architect must reconcile your equity budget with FHA, M. P. S., local building codes and LPA esthetics.

   (e) Architect must make sure that change orders are compensable in mortgage. Extras must not reduce mortgage, if variations or omissions. Must trade pluses for minuses, or get commitment for pluses.

   (f) Should assume responsibility for plan omissions causing extras which are not mortgageable.

14. <u>Special FHA problems with general contractor and subs:</u>

   (a) Shall you have a joint venture with a local G. C. ? <u>He</u> has local subs, local sources of supply, local union and building department contacts, local supervisory people and a local image.

   (b) <u>You</u> have better financial sources, more FHA and Urban Renewal experience, a more experienced legal, accounting and tax planning team.

   (c) Check out with your local contact, who can buy each item better: supplies; material; lumber; labor, etc.

   (d) Beware of the identity of interest problem. Be certain your venture is set up in such manner that you will qualify to get builders' and sponsors' profit and risk allowance. You cannot afford to lose that 10% fee because too much of your contracting work has been given out and it looks like there is no G. C. on the job who is entitled to receive the 10% fee. Check this item out carefully with your local FHA office before you give out all the contract work.

15. <u>Drawing your joint venture agreement:</u>

A carefully drawn joint venture agreement is indispensable. Who will do what? When? What risks will each assume? What are the obligations as to timing? Financing of each party? How will profits and losses, as well as tax benefits be shared?

Chapter IV

MORTGAGE FINANCING FOR YOUR PROJECT

Conventional Financing and How It Is Done

Most of our readers will know how to do this, but we are restating conventional apartment financing step by step so that we can contrast it with the FHA process in the succeeding pages.

A whole group of skills is required by the apartment house builder or developer. In a way, what you have learned on one project does not help you on the next. Each job involves unique and unusual problems in land acquisition, mortgage financing, layout and design, and construction. Even the most experienced developer will tell you that as he moves from job to job, problems which seemed easy on his last job become extremely difficult on this one. As a general rule, the more quickly the job moves, the fewer the problems which arise. If there is too great a time lag from land acquisition to rental of the finished job, money costs may change, construction costs may change, and over-building may evaporate your market.

Equity Financing—The Key

Our own experience has been that the better financing the developer has, the better off he is. A few dollars in the bank help the builder withstand tenant pressures, drive harder bargains with suppliers, hold his land site a little longer until he can get better zoning, await a turn in the mortgage market for financing, etc. The thinner, leaner and hungrier the builder, the less hope there is for his survival.

Our only advice to the talented, lean, hungry young man is to get himself a fat, placid partner with a good bank roll. Time heals even a sick job (although the return to your equity investor may not be as good). Since almost all apartment house ventures are set up with as little equity as possible—the leaner the bank roll, the less time you can afford to buy, and the less hope there is for survival.

Site Location

Assuming, then, you have the bank roll (your own or your mother-in-law's) you must begin by locating a piece of land. If you have been in the business for some time, you don't have to look for a piece of land—real estate brokers will be chasing you all the time, offering you "desirable" land sites. You will go over these and weigh one against the other. You will see if the land cost per apartment meets your requirements. You will ask yourself whether the site has tenant appeal and wonder whether it will have "romance" to mortgage lenders.

Good land is not cheap. Smart builders will pay top dollar for a site which is ripe. Only an amateur would buy an inexpensive site off the beaten path. The old cliché about location, location and location being the three most important factors in the real estate business is certainly true here. The wise builder pays top dollar for his land because experience has taught him that saving 25% on land cost cuts the final cost of the project by 5% or less. In most cases, land cost will not exceed 20% of the total project cost.

If you save a couple of dollars on land cost, but take six more months to rent up—what have you done for yourself? The loss of rental will be yours, as the developer; whereas the increased

60

land cost may come wholly out of the mortgage lender's pocket, since a desirable site should produce a larger loan from conventional lenders.

Buying the Land "Right"

The wise builder may pay top dollar for his land but he will generally try to work out maximum financing. He will try to get as long a purchase money mortgage as possible and put down as little cash as possible. In some cases, builders have even been able to convince sellers that they should put no cash into the deal. If the ultimate price is high, builders may be able to convince sellers that since the builders are going to spend considerable funds on plans, architectural specifications and re-zoning, all benefits which will inure to the seller, even if the builder flops, the seller should accept these costs in lieu of cash on contract. In some instances, the seller will take as little as 5% or 10% cash and give long-term purchase money mortgages, provided he does not have to subordinate to the construction loan. He knows full well he has little to lose and much to gain if the builder ultimately gets him the price he wants for the land.

While re-zoning, mortgaging and planning are carried on, the seller is relieved not only of the processing costs but the taxes and carrying charges while the builder is moving along.

Nonetheless, desirable land sites require considerable money, and often the seller wants all cash. Desirable New York City apartment locations have been known to approach $60, $70 and $100 per square foot; a 10,000 foot parcel (small, by today's standards) can conceivably run close to $1 million. It is a rare construction mortgage that will permit the builder to bail out that kind of land cost on the first payment, so his money remains tied up until project completion or renting.

Tax Considerations on Taking Title

The builder will have a decision to make on taking title to the land; he may want to take title in his own name, or in the name of his investment group, to get the tax savings which flow from interest, taxes and other carrying charges during the period of development. On the other hand, he may decide to put the mortgage in a corporate name and elect "Subchapter S" treatment to pass the losses through to himself. More about tax considerations in the final chapters of this book.

Hunting for a Conventional Mortgage

Once the land has been acquired, or after contract has been signed and before title has passed, the builder will begin work on mortgage financing. Preliminary plans and specifications are drawn by an architect for submission to various lending institutions and the developer (or his mortgage broker) prepares an analysis suitable for presentation to lending institutions showing the proposed costs, potential rentals, proposed layouts, room counts and generalized specifications.

A short leaflet, brochure or presentation will describe the neighborhood, schools, transportation, etc.; the appraised value of the land or the cost thereof, the size of the proposed mortgage loan and the proposed equity financing are stated. While lenders will not issue a meaningful commitment without architectural and financial presentations, mortgage brokers and professional developers who have borrowed many times generally have an idea of the kind of loan they can count on at a particular time, based on the number of cubic feet of construction and the rental potential.

Construction Money Against the Permanent Loan

Once a commitment for permanent financing has been issued by the potential lender, final plans will be drawn, bids will be taken from the various trades, and the developer will begin to look around for a construction loan (unless the construction money is also going to come from the permanent lender).

Getting together the required building plans and making arrangements for mortgage financing can take as little as three months, and as long as six or seven months, depending upon market conditions, the complexity of the job and the skill of the professionals working on the matter.

And Now Construction Starts

With land acquired, permanent and construction financing committed, plans filed and bid on, and contracts and subcontracts given out, demolition or foundation work begins. Of course, if the builder bought a presently occupied site, present tenants must be evicted when their leases expire. In situations where premises are rent-controlled (as in New York), many, many months may go by—as many as thirteen or fourteen—while the tenants make every possible appeal in their battle to stay in possession. Sites occupied by tenants not only have to take demolition costs and time into consideration, but the cost of buying up or evicting the tenants, plus the legal fees involved.

Timing Your Advances

Presumably, construction loan financing is tied to the needs of the builder's subcontractors, so that if all goes well, the rest of the job, after land acquisition, should be self-financing.

In other words, if all goes according to plan, the construction lender's payments at various stages of completion should match the needs and demands of the subcontractors, whose contracts should be tied to the construction loan progress-payment schedule. At least that is the theory. In practice, the failure of one sub to tie together his work with another sub, the bankruptcy or labor problems of one or more subs, slow or late delivery by material suppliers, labor disputes, mechanic's liens, weather conditions—and the Good Lord knows what have risen to plague builders since the Israelites left the Pyramids.

Meanwhile, interest and tax costs continue to come out of the builder's pocket and, unless he has made a very liberal construction loan financing arrangement, he runs short of cash. It is this need for cash which made us say at the beginning of this section that the successful builder either has substantial cash assets of his own or has a partner with cash. If he has neither, he fights with his subcontractors or holds back on their payments.

Using Subs to Finance
Your Job

While construction loan payments generally should carry the job to completion, most subcontractors do not get the full amount due them under their contract until the job is finished. There is a "hold back" of 10% to 20% which enables the builder to keep a little ahead of the subs, thereby financing the job. When the job is finished, the builder must come up with some more equity capital, unless his permanent loan is sufficiently large to make up that 10% to 20% difference.

Hopefully, the permanent loan should be large enough to pay off the construction loan, to return to the builder a substantial amount of the equity in his land, and to make enough extra cash to pay the subcontractors any remainders due them on the 10% to 20% hold back. However, this does not always work out.

Commitment for Variable Amounts
of Mortgage Loans

In tight mortgage markets or difficult renting markets, permanent mortgage loans are tied to specific rental schedules. If the building is only 60% rented at the time construction is finished, the permanent lender may be willing to make a loan of only 60% to 70% of the final loan. Pressure is thus exerted on the builder to get up the balance of the money or to rent up those vacant apartments. Once again, we see the need for adequate financing. The combined pressure of a weak rental market and a hard mortgage lender may force the builder to make unwise renting decisions or compel him to seek outside funds at usurious rates, unless he is adequately financed.

Effect of Money Shortage

Since actual construction work should take approximately a year, it may be 18 months from the time builder first took title to his land to his permanent mortgage on completion. It may be six months or a year later before the builder is _fully_ rented up, during which time his project may be operating at below the break-even point.

Another advantage of being well financed is the apartment developer's ability to "buy right." Generally speaking, full-time professional apartment developers not only act as their own general contractors, but may take on one of the sub-trades as well. Thus, a carpentry contractor who ultimately learns to become an apartment house developer may still do his own carpentry contracting work. The same is true of the plumbing, electrical and masonry contractors who may have become apartment house developers.

The well-financed developer is able to buy cheaper labor costs and make better material deals if he is ready to pay cash on the barrelhead, and even to finance the people who sell or work for him. The under-financed developer, by holding back on his subs, may get the financing he wants, but he's got to pay the price for it. As a captive buyer, he is unable to drive a hard bargain.

The under-financed builder must always ask himself whether he is better off giving up a piece of his equity to a "silent" financing partner, thereby making attendant savings in materials and labor, or whether he is better off without a financial partner, making the best deals he can with the trades who will charge him top dollar therefor in exchange for extended payment terms.

Renting

Selling or renting the apartments may have been partially done while the structure was going up, or it may not even start until the structure is pretty well finished. The builder, of course, would rather rent from models, but in a competitive rental market, customers clearly prefer renting in an existing building rather than go to one not yet completed.

Prospective tenants fear that the building may not be completed on time and that they may make arrangements to leave their old apartments before their new ones are ready. In a tight rental market, of course, where the demand exceeds the supply, it has been possible to rent from plans plus a model apartment or even from a hole in the ground.

The Conventional Timetable

Assuming the apartment is fully rented, the developer has now completed from 2-1/2 to 3 years of work. The timing starts from the moment the developer first begins negotiating for the piece of land and ends the day when he is fully rented up (and ready to re-sell the project or start collecting dividends from it). On paper in many cases it looks like he makes from 20% to 30% a year on his money. In fact, that computation does not take into consideration any pay for the years of training our developer has had nor for the "sweat" equity he has put into the job in terms of negotiating the land contract, negotiating mortgage financing, planning layouts and working with the architect, sweating out the financing, fighting with the suppliers and subcontractors, carrying out the sales plan and marketing the apartments.

If all is well, our builder-developer has the satisfaction of seeing a good-looking, finished job, fully rented, on which he has made a good return on his capital. He is ready to go on to the next job with the hope that it will go a little faster, be a little easier, and that he will make a few more percentage points on his investment next time.

Why Push for the
Highest Mortgage?

To begin with, most builders are chronically underfinanced. They would like to build as large a project as possible with as small a cash equity as possible. This enables them to do more projects and to make a higher return on their money. It also transfers a major portion of the risk to the mortgage lender.

Let us look at a few figures which demonstrate the importance of mortgage leverage and the reason why most Urban Renewal borrowers and many multi-family developers turn to FHA financing since mortgages of up to 90% are available. Other FHA benefits, of course, are the longer term mortgages offered with lower annual amortization charges resulting in lower debt service. Finally, under the FHA programs, it is possible to reinvest your builder's fee "so 97% financing may be available."

Let us look at the effect of mortgage leverage on a $1 million project which makes $100,000 a year on a free and clear basis (before paying anything out to service the mortgage debt). Let us assume three different loans: a $600,000 loan; an $800,000 loan and a $900,000 loan. Let us further assume that 8% constant would be required for debt service with 6-1/2% allocated to interest, and 1-1/2% to mortgage amortization. Obviously, in the realities of the market place, the $600,000 loan would probably command a lower interest rate since it is a more conservative one, but we have kept all the figures on a comparable basis here, since we are trying to illustrate the importance of leverage, and leverage alone.

Leverage at Work
$1 million project—$100,000 free and clear cash flow

Amount of mortgage		
$900,000	$800,000	$600,000
requires for debt service (at 8% constant)		
$ 72,000	$ 64,000	$ 48,000
leaves a net cash flow to the equity investor, after debt service of		
$ 28,000	$ 36,000	$ 52,000
on an equity investment of		
$100,000	$200,000	$400,000
or a net return on cash equity of		
28%	18%	13%

Developing an FHA Apartment Job

In many respects, the FHA and conventional jobs are similar. As a matter of fact, in many cases, the potential conventional loan may not be much smaller than the potential FHA loan. While the FHA loan may go to 90% of the certified construction and land costs, conventional financing goes to two-thirds of "value." Value may be substantially higher than costs for the builder who is able to effectuate substantial savings in construction and who has bought a fine piece of land at the right price.

Why FHA at All, Then?

It is reasonable to assume that the efficient builder will always ask himself whether he can do a conventional loan first, before going near the FHA. The piece of land sought for conventional financing may not be suitable for FHA financing and vice versa; but if it looks like the loan might go either way, most builders choose to use conventional financing, since time is money and since FHA processing and red tape take time.

It is true that the FHA has improved its processing and now takes less time than it used to take, but even the FHA does not contend that it takes less time or less red tape to do an FHA loan rather than a conventional one.

Let us assume that the builder has decided to do an FHA job rather than a conventional one. If that be the case, instead of first picking out a land site and then getting an analysis of possible construction costs and rental values coupled with an architectural plan, the FHA builder knows that since the FHA is putting up the bulk of the financing, he had better go to them first.

FHA Site Approval

In an FHA job, since the builder is counting on FHA financing running from 90% to 100%, he knows he is going to have to satisfy the FHA's needs and demands. His relationship to the FHA is very much like the relationship of a general contractor (in a conventional job) to the equity owner. In other words, it is the FHA which calls the shots. FHA will deny this. They will tell you that it is the developer who must make the decisions—but just try to do it.

Pick out a piece of land in an area which the FHA thinks is "too far out" or tell them that you can find a market where their market studies say "there is none," and then try to sell them the job. The conventional builder can, in many cases, get permanent financing once he has demonstrated he is right and the lender is wrong merely by "renting up" during the construction loan period. But the FHA borrower never gets that chance, unless he wants to build free and clear and then take his job to FHA for processing after it is finished. Even if this were possible, such a plan is absurd.

Since the developer has delegated the real decision making about location, market and even specifications to the FHA, he spends most of his time trying to keep as little of his own equity as possible in the job. Then the funds as well as the decisions can come from the FHA.

Within reason, cost savings mean little to FHA builders since they will reduce the mortgage proceeds on certification. What is important to the FHA developer is that he put as little of his own money in the job as possible. Since the developer knows he is dealing with FHA controls of all sorts, with all kinds of red tape, he wants to be in a position to walk away from the job if his arm is twisted to the point where it is broken and bleeding.

If he has done his job right, he has little or no dollar equity in the final job, and his concern as to whether the job rents or not and how long it stays rented is minimized.

It is true that under modern practice, the builder may need a letter of credit or performance bond which will carry him through the renting-up process, but presumably, he has been adequately compensated in his land mark-up, his builder's fee, his tax shelter and other incentives. Of course, all the work is for naught under cost certification since there can be no builder's profit in a foreclosure. The builder may have no risk, but he can make no money unless he rents up.

Sounding Out FHA

In any event, the technique of doing an FHA job starts with going to the local FHA office to "feel them out" about land costs and locations as well as their analysis of the market in garden versus high-rise, in room layouts and sizes, room costs and amenities, etc. In other words, the FHA builder is asking his mortgage insurer what will pass muster—the builder is not telling the insurer what he plans to do, he is asking.

Again, to minimize his financial commitment, the FHA builder, instead of buying land, will try to option it or take a long-term contract involving as small an outlay of equity capital as possible. He wants to keep his equity capital down; he does not want to buy the land unless he can be sure of getting an FHA insurance commitment.

Minimizing Your Investment

The builder who has had FHA experience realizes that since his total land cost must bear the required relationship to the total cost of the structure, the land must not contain unusual blasting, foundation, excavating or other abnormal site processing costs. The FHA is not likely to grant credit for those site problems in its mortgage. Also, the FHA builder must not have substantial expenditures for off-site improvements such as electric, gas, telephone, sewer, water connections or roads, streets, access ways, etc., since these off-site improvements may not be permitted as part of the mortgage cost, either.

The FHA builder will have his architect (presumably one familiar with FHA requirements, specifications and processing) prepare a preliminary set of plans which must meet not only municipal building regulations, but FHA's minimum property specifications, room count requirements, etc.

The Architect's Design Problems

The architect will specify nothing which will not bring credit on an FHA mortgage, and in many cases, the architect will work on "speculation." That is, he will prepare his plans on speculation, especially if he has confidence in the builder, since the architect knows he will get paid out of the FHA mortgage proceeds just as the builder gets paid.

FHA construction is not a place to "make waves." The tried and tested ways which have been processed many times through FHA offices before, are the ones that will generally speed through most quickly. The builder who has a novel and experimental design will require more time for processing. He who innovates must break open doors, and conventional lenders have thinner doors than governmental ones.

The Money Market Problems

Since the FHA itself makes no mortgage loans, the builder must simultaneously be seeking a mortgage lender. If money is hard to get, lenders may not want to commit themselves to make loans at standard FHA rates and may require the builder to pay "points," which means to take the mortgage in at less than par with the result that the discount will come out of the builder's pocket and increase his equity investment. When mortgage money is easy to get, lenders may fight for FHA loans and may even offer

70

substantial inducements to builders who bring them such loans. In any event, the developer obtains a letter from the proposed mortgage lender stating that when, as, and if he obtains an FHA mortgage insurance commitment, the lender will make the permanent loan. It is now possible for the FHA to insure construction loans, so the developer may get from the same lender (or a different lender) a tentative commitment to make the construction advances.

Additional Steps

Assuming that the land has been tied down by an option or a contract, the preliminary plans have been accepted by the FHA, that the developer has submitted and had accepted an analysis of the cost of the proposed project and the proposed rental schedule, that he has found a tentative mortgage lender and a tentative construction lender, that the developer has specific details on the materials and labor required in the job—he is ready to apply for and get a formal commitment from the FHA. In a normal FHA market a skilled builder with an informed architect may have taken six to eight weeks from the time they first chatted with the FHA, and found out the project and the location were okay, to the time they obtained a letter of feasibility stating FHA is ready to go ahead toward a formal commitment. More detailed plans and documentation are required; specifications must be clarified either by the investor or his architect, and if there's anything unusual about the job, the district office may check with the regional office or Washington. Finally, a 90-day commitment for mortgage insurance will be issued and an additional three or four months will have elapsed.

Market Changes

During the past five to six months the market may have changed; construction costs may vary or the money market may have become very difficult. The builder can still pull away and all he loses is his work, plus the architect's and legal fees involved and the commitment fees he has laid out.

If he's ready to move along, however, he now files for a building permit, takes title to his land, gets any necessary zoning matters straightened out, sets up a corporation to build the job under the FHA's standard charter, and gives out his construction contracts.

In the meantime, he has been sharpening up the FHA's agreement to rent schedules (both projected and actual and hypothetical maximum rents) and he is now ready to go to his first formal "closing" with the FHA—which means he will obtain a final commitment for mortgage insurance from the FHA and his first payment thereunder from his lender.

Formal Closing

The first formal FHA closing can be a complicated legal affair with many lawyers present representing the investor, regional office of FHA, lender's lawyers, title company people, etc. It's the first time the builder sees any money and, with luck, the first closing may begin part of a series of payments that will ultimately bail him out.

Shortly thereafter, construction will start and FHA construction, because of inspection problems, may take from three to six months longer than conventional construction, so that a typical FHA job may take between 12 and 18 months instead of the 12 months which a typical conventional job may come in at.

When construction is completed and a certificate of occupancy has been issued, the FHA will place its final endorsement on the mortgage note and the permanent mortgage loan closed, provided the builder has had certified accounting statement prepared and examined by the FHA to prevent his "bailing out" more than his actual cost. Under today's conditions, the builder may have no cash in the job at this point—or very little, depending on which of the FHA sections govern the loan.

Builder Guarantees

The developer may have a letter of credit or other guarantee around assuring the FHA that interest and carrying charges will be taken care of for a fixed period estimated by the FHA as being required to rent up the job. Hopefully, it will only take a year to rent up the job, at which point the developer is in the clear, having obtained all his mortgage payments and being "off the hook" as far as any letter of credit or other rental guarantee is concerned. The time from beginning to end on the FHA project may possibly be a year longer than the conventional job. If a conventional job can be done in three years, the FHA won't be finished until four years.

72

Chapter V

UNDERSTANDING THE WHY'S AND WHEREFORE'S OF FHA

The Thinking Behind
FHA Programs

Over a drink, after a home builders' convention, a key FHA official admitted to a small group of professionals, "I spend a third of my time preparing for congressional hearings, in trying to convince Congress that there will be no multi-family housing program unless we can liberalize loans to builders. Then, I spend a third of my time selling the FHA's lending programs to builders and demonstrating to them how they can make money with the program. Finally, I go back to my office and spend the other third of my time devising ways to prevent builders from making 'too much money' in the programs, so I can avoid having to appear before Congress once again to explain away another set of scandals."

That about sums it up. Builders cannot go through the time-consuming paper work of FHA, nor will they surrender their ability to make their own management decisions on land location, room layout and amenities if they can get liberal, conventional financing in similar amounts. Conventional financing moves many times as fast, and attaches fewer strings.

Why FHA, Then?

On the other hand, when an FHA program permits a builder to own a sizable development with little or no cash investment of his own, or when a program offers the opportunity to make six and seven figure builder's fees and then sell the job to a co-op, builders will flock to the program.

As builders flock, there will be some abuses, since a program which assures a profit without thrusting on the builder the burden of finding a market holds romance for the get-rich-quick builder. A profitable program also attracts the used car dealer who was always dreaming of getting into the building business, plus a large group of lawyers, accountants, brokers, architects and others who see the opportunity of making a large profit in exchange for some time-consuming paper work.

The Safeguards
(Also Called Bureaucratic "Red Tape")

Having had many years of experience with this phenomenon and having been subjected to congressional investigation and pressure, the FHA has devised a number of safeguards—some administratively and some by way of congressional fiat.

It is the purpose of this section to deal with some of those controls. In the main, today's FHA controls lie largely in the fields of cost certification, equity controls and rental increase restrictions. Depending on the program, the FHA regulates cash investments, rates of return, rentals, capital structure, accounting procedures, replacement reserves, design and construction requirements and interest rates on multi-family housing projects. Not only is FHA a partner (in some of the programs the FHA holds preferred stock), but it functions much like a public utility regulatory agency in fixing rates of return and rental charges.

In exchange for these regulatory devices, the FHA gives to the developer an opportunity to raise mortgage money at more favorable terms than the conventional lender will give him. Whenever the mortgage market gets soft and conventional lenders compete to press large loans on builders, the FHA program languishes. Many of the FHA restrictions we deal with exist only in the multi-family program and not in the one-family home field

74

where the FHA may give even more highly leveraged loans. However, no one seems to care, since the benefit of these loans goes to the buyer and not to the builder.

Some of the Controls

The FHA-developer conflict starts early in the history of a multi-family housing loan. Aside from administrative controls, Congress has imposed loan to value limits, total mortgage loan per project limits, per dwelling unit and per room limits, and a limit on maximum interest rates.

Administratively, the FHA has reasonably liberal powers to increase multi-family housing loans in "high cost areas" and, through its discretionary powers, effectively has acquired control over the amount of equity capital needed for a particular project.

Such controls as the rental schedule, the net return formula, "cost certification," regulatory agreements, replacement reserves, profit distribution controls, maintenance requirements, default controls or waivers, and the right to waive or postpone interest and amortization, are all within the administrative control of the FHA.

The Short-Term View of FHA

Since these administrative controls determine whether a particular project shall prosper or die, and since the administrative body itself is subject to changes of political administration and to congressional criticism, most developers take a jaundiced view of FHA over the long-term. Builders will enter an FHA multi-family program only if the short-term benefits are there.

The key short-term decisions which either interest developers in an FHA program or make them run from it, start at the mortgage commitment level.

"How much cash am I going to have to put into the job, and how long will I have to keep it there?" That is the key question every FHA developer asks himself as he approaches FHA on a new multi-family project. Developers can learn to live with FHA red tape, with inspections, with specifications, with layout and design controls, but they will not go near a program which requires a substantial long-term cash investment. Knowing that in the long term they will be subject to administrative whims and capital controls, developers are attracted to an FHA program only by the hope of "mortgaging out," or the hope of owning something which is salable or tax deductible which requires little or no cash investment of their own. All the rest is mumbo jumbo.

The FHA's View

Experience with the § 608 and other liberal mortgage programs has made the FHA chary of builders who grow plump merely by building the project, without having any interest in the renting or future thereof. As a result, programs may languish or flourish based on whether the builder is able to make a "land profit" in "selling" his parcel to a multi-family co-op.

Since all the multi-family programs are highly leveraged, the difference between a 95% loan and a 98% or 100% loan can be the difference between a program's moving or languishing.

In many cases, Congress has found it politically unpalatable to make 100% loans, and accordingly, limits most loan programs to 90%. If the programs do not flourish, they may permit a 10% "builder's risk allowance" which will mean, on a realistic basis, that a mortgage of close to 100% can exist. On the other hand, in fairness to Congress' position, experience has shown that without controls, developers will enthusiastically build high-rise apartment projects 7,000 miles from the nearest railroad station in the depths of Alaska's tundras, provided they can make a land profit on the deal.

Requiring the builder to have as little as 1% or 2% of his own money in the job may prevent a multi-million dollar scandal. It has been stated that cost certification has penalized the efficient builder and rewarded the amateur, by reducing the mortgage loan of the efficient builder and encouraging less efficient amateurs.

On the other hand, the FHA § 608 program, which permitted professionals to "mortgage out" while inexperienced newcomers owned their jobs with little or no equity, raised problems all of its own. As an FHA representative testified before the United States Senate Banking and Currency Committee:

Up to the advent of the 608 program no apartment houses
in New Orleans were larger than 20 or 25 units. When the
608 program started, we were instructed, and indeed
urged by Washington, to sell the 608 program to builders to
provide badly needed rental housing. We went out and we did
a good selling job. We did too good a selling job. Over 5,800
units of rental housing came onto the market in New Orleans
within a period of approximately 18 months to 2 years—and it
was just a little more than we could absorb at one time.

Some of the rental projects wound up with vacancy rates of 80% and
90%! At the end of five or six years, 18 New Orleans projects—
nearly 50% of the total that had been built—were back in FHA hands.

Yet, despite the waste, the FHA's 608 program did get an
amazing amount of rental housing built in a very short time. No
public housing program could have produced results so fast, nor
is it certain that the total cost of bureaucratic housing would have
been less, if all had been built by Public Housing Authorities
(with their own red tape) but with no foreclosures.

As a result of 608 experience, the FHA now makes an effort,
in most of its programs, to see that the builder has 2-1/2% to 3%
of his own money in the job, over and above all his certified costs.

FHA Regulation of the "Finished"
Apartment House

A major area of annoyance with the FHA multi-family housing program comes out of the controls FHA imposes, in exchange
for its liberal mortgage loan, even after the project is completed.
For a while the FHA controlled its projects through a model
charter, which it required the borrower to insert in his corporate
documents. Now that the FHA permits (for tax reasons) individuals,
partnerships and trusts to become borrowers, it has taken most of
the regulatory provisions which formerly were found in the corporate charter and put them in a regulatory agreement which becomes
part of the mortgage. The controls found in the regulatory agreement cover almost every important managerial decision operating
the property.

The major gripe of multi-family developers is that the FHA's
single-family home ownership program contains no such regulatory

agreements. The FHA does not require the one-family home purchaser under a "no down payment" mortgage to "adequately maintain" his property. The one-family home owner does not have to make any deposit into a replacement reserve fund. The one-family home owner is not restricted as to any "profit" he may make either on re-sale or on renting.

On the other hand, we must face political realities. FHA is able to point out that every one of its fears, every one of the regulations included in its multi-family regulatory agreement, has been justified by its experience in one project or another or in one program or another. Regulatory and charter provisions are broad, and unfortunately, the FHA moves neither quickly enough nor uniformly enough to satisfy many investor-developers.

FHA Rental Controls

For many years it was not clear under what conditions FHA would permit rent increases, since the charters themselves merely stated "no increases in charges from the approved rental schedule shall be made except with the consent of the FHA." Lack of uniformity from office to office also increased irritation. Thus, investors with successful projects hoped they would be able to pass along cost increases to their tenants on lease renewals. If a project rented well, and did not need its 7% vacancy allowance, investors found in many cases that the FHA felt they should absorb the cost increases to some extent out of the vacancy allowance and not pass the increases along to the tenants. This irritated investors, particularly those who had held property for a number of years and who had experienced higher than 7% vacancy allowances in earlier years. The FHA, they complained, did not permit them to make up for the bad years in the good ones.

The experience was not uniform in all offices, and it took some time until Washington straightened this matter out. But investors today fear that there may come a time again when the FHA, subjected to local political pressures, may refuse to give the investor his due.

Dividend Regulation by FHA

In addition to FHA regulation of rental schedules, investors are exasperated by FHA supervision over the payment of dividends to themselves, as investors. The typical multi-family apartment house developer wants his equity out of the apartment project as quickly as possible, so he can get it at work on another job.

"Why," he asks, "should I be penalized and have to lock my money into a project if I am efficient and rent up quickly? If I am making a return, keeping the project up, paying all of my FHA requirements and depositing my reserve—why can't I pull the money out as quickly as I want?"

For a time, particularly in the corporate borrower program, the FHA required that 30% of the total book value of the equity had to be locked into "irredeemable common stock." It is true that the FHA did permit the investor to use surplus cash to pay down his mortgage, but this is a far cry from giving the investor the right to put the projects in his own pocket. Turning money over to the FHA is not the same thing as drawing it out for your own benefit.

Replacement Reserves

The practice of FHA multi-family housing projects is to require that the investor segregate each month a specific amount of cash to be used for replacement of those parts of the building which wear out or for necessary capital alterations. In a way, FHA's concern that there be money to make major capital repairs is a justifiable one. The FHA had reason to fear that thinly capitalized investors might "cream off" the profits in the early years (when replacements were minimal) and walk away from the job as the building got older. Since the FHA is tied to forty-year mortgages, they could not permit investors to "milk" the building and walk away.

Investors can understand the requirement for building up this reserve, but they are concerned with the rigidity with which the FHA approaches the problem. At least on paper, since the amount of the reserve is a matter for administrative discretion for the FHA, it is entirely possible—on paper—for the reserve to accumulate to over 10%, especially when interest begins to accumulate.

Such a reserve would be manifestly too high and the difficulty of getting funds released from the reserve for re-investment in the project is another investor gripe.

Finally, the build-up of this cash reserve creates tax problems for the investor because although the reserve is not cash flow which can pass through to the investor, the investor gets no tax deduction for his abstinence. The amounts put in the cash reserve account are not considered expenses for federal income tax purposes, so that the investor is in the position of paying a tax on money he is not able to use for 40 years.

Restrictions on Rents and Profits

FHA rental controls are more a matter of administrative practice than congressional requirement. Since the FHA is politically sensitive to tenant pressures by local congressmen, this makes investor-developers worry. There can be no certainty that the liberal administrative procedures of today won't be replaced by arbitrary procedures tomorrow.

Nonetheless, Returns Can Exceed 40% a Year

It is true that on paper the FHA's technique of fixing rental ceilings provides the possibility of a liberal return on investments. Although the exact formula has varied from program to program, rents are usually fixed at a rate sufficient to cover all operating costs, real estate taxes, debt service, payments to the replacement reserve plus a 7% vacancy allowance and a return of approximately 12% on original book equity.

If 100% occupancy can be achieved, the return on book equity can go to 20% and if cash equity (after allowing for builder's fees which involve no cash investment) is only half of book equity, it is possible to have a return on cash investment of as much as 40% or even higher. We do not know of many projects which achieved that result, but one can see that on paper, at least, the rent formula is reasonably liberal. (For some examples of how this is done, see our first chapter). In addition there are income tax benefits which are discussed elsewhere.

As we mentioned before, the problem of the rent formula is that it hangs over the project. While operating costs remain stable there is usually little conflict. However, as real property taxes and operating costs begin to rise, if the investor's return is to be protected, the FHA must permit the owner to pass along rent increases to the tenants as quickly as possible. Since tenants have leases, even the speediest action by FHA will not permit the owner to recoup all of his cost increases. If the FHA wants to take time and audit all the books before granting increases, if it wants to decide whether all increases are justifiable—to seek to take the increases out of the vacancy allowance, etc., etc.—the owner can be badly hung up while the FHA dawdles with its own red tape or decides that it is politically wiser to side with tenants than with landlords.

Why Penalize Know-How?

The owner who has picked a very desirable location and built a better-than-average project cannot get increases merely because his apartments are desirable. Rentals are permanently tied to the original capital value of the project.

The only hope of freedom for the owner is to pay off his FHA mortgage and shake loose from FHA controls entirely.

Again, the multi-family investor feels discriminated against. One-family home owners are not subjected to this kind of regulation, nor are multi-family owners who buy their own co-ops. The investor justifiably points out that he is being deprived of one of the major advantages of his highly leveraged investment; the opportunity to cash in on long-term inflation.

If the owner is always going to have his return locked into the cost of the project at the time it was built, what attractiveness has the project for re-sale? The rent control program is subject to the further criticism that its controls may not even make social sense.

Let us take two FHA projects setting opposite each other on a street. One was built in 1950; the other in 1960. The 1950 project cost $1 million; the 1960 one cost $1-1/4 million. Why should the tenants of the 1950 project be assured of rents approximately 25% lower than those in the 1960 project?

Since the tenancy of the 1950 building may have turned over three or four times since it was built, we are not even protecting the original tenants.

If the free market were permitted to operate, it seems clear that the 1950 project would begin to creep up on the 1960 project and both would find their own rental levels, thus forcing the 1960 project rentals down somewhat (to compete with the 1950 job) and permitting the 1950 owner to get some increases.

Obviously, what now happens is that the owners of older projects, which have had substantial mortgage amortization and which are well located, can get rent increases outside the FHA program and seek to free themselves from FHA by re-financing conventionally. The only projects which remain in the FHA-insured program will be those which cannot compete on their merits in the conventional loan market. The investor will not permit the FHA to penalize him, if he has any hope of re-financing with a conventional loan.

By preventing rent increases, the developer is penalized in his attempt to re-sell his project at a capital gain. As long as FHA ceilings prevent rental increases, FHA projects will sell at lower prices than conventionally-financed and uncontrolled apartments.

Checklist of Benefits and Controls

We have prepared a developer's checklist, to be used in checking out the controls of the particular FHA program in which you contemplate engaging. You will find this appendix useful in comparing one FHA program with other governmentally insured programs, such as Mitchell-Lama in New York State, or Local Assistance or Urban Renewal financing available in other states.

After giving you the checklist, now that we have explained the theory behind FHA administrative and statutory controls, we are ready to begin discussion of the processing techniques. In other words, the next chapter will take you step by step through FHA processing, beginning with your initial conference and running through your final payments under the mortgage.

DEVELOPER'S CHECKLIST ON THE BENEFITS, CONTROLS AND PROCESSING OF THIS PARTICULAR PROGRAM

1. What's in it for the developer?

(a) Builder's fee;

(b) Land profit; or

(c) Income on a long-term investment basis.

2. <u>Why this program instead of a conventional job</u>?

    (a) Financing benefits and income benefits;

    (b) Competitive advantages in the market place (lower rents; marketability) economics.

3. <u>Financing benefits</u>:

    (a) How high a mortgage loan?

    (b) Can you invest your "builder's fee" in lieu of cash;

    (c) What kind of construction loan can you get and will the agency help you get one? How long will it run, and what will it cost?

    (d) Does the program require any specific amount of equity capital to be invested in the job when completed?

4. <u>What kind of return can be earned on equity? On cash investment</u>?

5. <u>Real estate tax abatement or reduction</u>:

    (a) Does the program require tax abatement? Can it be used with tax abatement? How is the tax abatement application handled (does the agency help)—what protection is there against changes in assessed valuation once the project is completed?

6. <u>Fees and allowances</u>:

    (a) What builder's fees are allowed? What architect's fees (as a percentage); what overhead allowances for builders; what legal and organizational fees; what rental commissions, management fees and leasing commissions after completion?

    (b) If the program is an insured one (as distinguished from a directly financed one), are mortgage brokerage or placement commissions allowable? Are commitment fees?

7. <u>Explore some examples of successful projects in the program and some examples of flops</u>:

    (a) Try to define the reasons for the successes and for the flops.

8. Is the program restricted to multi-family residential, or can it be used for commercial, industrial or office?

9. Can any of the loan be used to finance non-residential building, if in connection with the residential portion? If so, what are the limitations on commercial use?

10. Controls:

    (a) Cost certification: What does it mean to your job?
    (b) The subcontractor problem, if any: Must there be an identity of interest?

11. Format:

    (a) Must the ultimate owner be a corporation or can it be a partnership, real estate trust or individual (for income tax benefits)?

12. Land ownership:

    (a) Must the developer own the land when he first begins processing or is it enough to have an option?

13. Other agencies:

    (a) What other agencies (aside from yours) are required to clear the project (City agencies; Tax Commission, City Planning, etc., and other federal, state and local agencies)?

14. Design standards and other controls such as limitations:

    (a) Type limitations (i.e., only co-ops, only single families, etc.);
    (b) How do these design standards compare with conventional work (room sizes, locations, fireproof vs. non-fireproof, minimum number of rooms, amenity limitations, swimming pools, air conditioning, etc.)?

15. Some typical figures:

    (a) What kind of land cost makes sense in the program— per acre, per apartment and per room?

(b) What kind of location factors are important for the success of your kind of project?

(c) What are the construction cost limitations on the project?

16. Removal from control:

(a) Can you get out of the program after the job is finished; and, if so, when?

(b) Ability to re-finance conventionally.

(c) What kind of minimum capital requirement must be kept in the job after completion?

(d) Dividend and/or pay-out prohibitions on earnings after completion;

(e) Rent control limitations after completion;

(f) Replacement reserve requirements;

(g) Ability to release replacement reserves—when and what for?

(h) Construction controls; inspection—cost certification;

(i) Anti-speculation provisions: Can you sell the job at a profit, and, if so, when?

17. Practical problems:

(a) Why is the program not more popular in this area?

(b) What are its practical limitations and what can be done to overcome them?

18. Relief:

(a) If the job rents slowly, what kind of interest and amortization waivers can you get and what will you have to give up to get them?

19. Market:

(a) Generally, what rent range do these projects fall into?

(b) Are those rentals competitive with conventional programs?

(c) Are they competitive with other governmental financing programs?

20. Equity:

(a) What kind of equity must the developer have? Must

he post a bond or letter of credit to assure renting? How much and for how long?

(b) Where will the working capital come from? What kind of equity money should a realistic sponsor visualize he will need, from the start of the job through construction to the time when the job is finished?

(c) Do those requirements depend on the sponsor's ability or are they built into the program by administrative controls?

21. Processing and timing:

(a) What is a realistic timetable—from the time you first walk into the administrator's office until the time you get final approval to begin construction?

(b) What will be the time lag between the time you complete construction and the time you get your last mortgage check?

(c) What facts or documents are required to close out the final payment check?

22. Paper work:

(a) Go through the program step by step, from the first initial paper to the initial indication of interest, to approval of plans and starting of the project—through inspection—through cost certification program—through the interim payments while constructing—through renting and your administrative requirements—through the last payment.

23. What kind of paper work must be submitted when processing begins (i. e., architectural, legal, forms, etc.)?

24. Must you do your own market survey or does the agency do it?

(a) What kind of money must be laid out by the developer on paper work before he knows whether he has a deal that interests the agency or not?

25. Ask the agency for suggestions to speed up paper work.

26. What is the commonest fault or omission in the material sent to the agency by developers?

27. What are the commonest problems developers face when they go to the agency, and what tips does the agency have to speed up your paper work?

28. What kind of mortgage loan will be made and on what interest and amortization terms?

29. What kind of return will be permitted to the builder on his equity and will he be able to draw it out?

Chapter VI

THE PRACTICAL PROBLEMS
AND BENEFITS OF FHA
FINANCING.

This chapter is a blend of observations and practical tips that have come from my own experience, from clients, and from Messrs. John Maylott and Ralph Lapidula, the two most recent Chief Underwriters of the multi-family housing programs of FHA's New York office. Please do not consider anything in this chapter as FHA's official position, particularly since the chapter is a melange of the observations of all of us, since you can be certain that both Messrs. Maylott and Lapidula know the FHA's rules and regulations, and since they are the first persons we go to if we have a problem.

One last word of warning: Regulations and programs change from time to time and, indeed, despite FHA's effort to insure uniform practices from office to office, they do differ occasionally in different regions. Accordingly, you will want to check out the observations made here in your own FHA office and on your own project, at the time you are processing your own application. Nonetheless, we have tried to keep the processing discussion in this chapter on a broad and practical enough basis to be applicable to almost any program anywhere in the country, even though the forms, the timing and the techniques, as well as the requirements of any particular program, may change from time to time.

Do Your Homework and Do It Early

Since the entire key to Urban Renewal and FHA processing is to cut the time lag between the time you start the job to the time you finally get your money, you must do everything possible to cut the timetable. You should surround yourself with the best professional know-how you can get, and you should do as much preliminary study as you can before you even walk into the FHA.

FHA efficiency studies have shown that most of the time lag is caused by the builder and his professional advisors. For example, FHA often makes recommendations as to architectural changes and then the plans lie around in the architect's office for three weeks until the changes are made. Then it is not the FHA's fault if final approval comes three weeks later than had been expected.

FHA's Duties

FHA is primarily an insuring office. Everyone knows it makes no direct loans. All it does is to satisfy itself that the project is feasible and that it fits the statutory and administrative formulae, and then FHA issues a commitment. All the commitment does is to put FHA's official endorsement or guarantee on the back of either a construction loan or a permanent loan (or both). Before the commitment is issued, a great deal of work must be done by the FHA office and by the builder's team. It is the purpose of this and the following chapters to outline that work and how it can be speeded up.

The major function of this chapter will be to lay out in advance some of the problems that arise out of FHA mortgages so that you can think the problems through in your planning and in assembling your team.

If you have thought through these problems before visiting the FHA office and signing a contract to buy land, many hours of grief and thousands of dollars may be saved.

Why Use FHA At All?

FHA understands that most builders go into the FHA either because no conventional loan is available at all or because FHA will provide a larger loan or a longer amortization period—or for all three of those benefits. Also, FHA's § 221(d)(3) program offers a 3% interest rate and 39-year loans on new construction. Obviously, there is no conventional 3% money around on 39-year loans. Indeed, there is no 3% money around for 30 days. So, if you want some of these benefits, you will have to decide whether they are worth the paper work and FHA controls involved. Similarly, programs like the 1% interest rate offered home renters and buyers under § 235 and 236 require FHA processing.

Obviously, many builders have discovered that the benefits are greater than the cost of getting them, or none of us would be using the FHA program. It is up to you to decide for yourself whether your particular project needs the benefits offered and whether you are prepared to pay therefor by assuming the burdens of the administrative controls. These chapters will help you weigh the pluses with the minuses.

Timing Problems

Some years ago, a study of processing in the New York FHA office found that the average waiting time during which the FHA had to wait for papers to come back from either the sponsor, his architect or lawyer, came to almost 300 days.

Any time which the builder, his architect or lawyer can lop off those 300 days of waiting time is going to be time saved for the builder. Time is money in this kind of construction. During the last several years, FHA has undergone one paper-work reorganization after another, so that at the present time it expects to get multi-family housing loans out of its offices in as little as 30 days (See our discussion of AMP, Chapter VII).

That timetable, however, assumes efficient FHA processing on your part. If you are going to add your 300 working days to the FHA's 30 days it will still take you over a year to get out of FHA, because you are dragging your own feet. If you want optimum timing, your entire team must be on the ball. This means familiarizing yourself with FHA regulations and having long, intensive chats before you start processing, so that everyone knows what is expected of him. Each member of your team must understand that time is money and that papers cannot sit around in his office.

Assembling the Expert Team

In addition to your own builder or development organization, you should have on your side an accountant (who is familiar with FHA forms and cost certification procedure), an attorney with similar qualifications, and an architect with the same skills.

Indeed, if the job is large enough or out of your home territory, you may need two architects just as you may need two lawyers.

You may need one architect for design purposes and overall Urban Renewal skills and another architect for his specialized knowledge of local building codes and building administration matters.

For the same reason you may need two or more lawyers, one with local know-how and another with FHA and Urban Renewal skills. Either the lawyer or the accountant (or both of them) should also understand the tax problems and lending problems involved in Urban Renewal and FHA.

The Architect

One of the first problems you will have, once you have decided who your architect is going to be, is how to modify the A.I.A. Standard Architectural Hiring Form. Frankly, if you are going to use FHA financing, FHA has its own special architectural requirements and the standard A.I.A. Architectural Form will require so many modifications that it generally should not be used.

The architect must spend much of his time coordinating with local authorities and other professional personnel, and he will have to be paid in accordance with FHA requirements, and not standard A.I.A. requirements. Of course, you can, if you want, pay his fee out of your own pocket, but most developers expect FHA reimbursement for this cost (out of the mortgage proceeds).

Another FHA requirement is that the architect must be independent. In other words, the architectural firm cannot be a dummy for the builder; nor can the architect "kick back" to the builder. Cost certification just will not permit it. The FHA has its own standard schedule of architectural fees (which vary from locality to locality) just as it has a schedule covering legal and organizational fees. All of these fees, if they comply with FHA standards, can be charged off to the cost of the job under the mortgage, and reimbursed as part of the mortgage loan.

Reconciling FHA and Other Requirements

One of the key problems that your team will have will be to tie together FHA's property and lending requirements with local building, zoning and fire requirements, and, if the project is going to be in an Urban Renewal area, to tie together your plans with those of the redevelopment plan.

The architect will want to make certain that the plans he files will not only clear the local building authorities and pass zoning muster, but also qualify for the maximum bedroom count, for mortgage purposes, permitted by the FHA.

In other words, the architect will want to make sure that he gets you reimbursed for anything that costs money, wherever possible. FHA room counts have always been an ephemeral thing to all but the eye of the expert. In the past, a partition between two rooms or the provision of a patio or balcony could make the difference between being able to finance a project with a substantial mortgage or having the project fall apart as unmortgageable. Some of these room counts have now been simplified. Your FHA-wise architect will be in contact with the local FHA architectural office constantly to be sure that his plans are within the minimum property standards of FHA and that they are producing the maximum FHA mortgage loan.

Your architect will also be coordinating his plans with you to make certain that they are producing a product which is marketable.

Finally, the architect's plans will have to be coordinated with the demands of the Urban Renewal people, to achieve esthetic results. In truth, no architect could ever accomplish all of these objectives; but a good one balances them to the greatest extent he

can and leaves final decisions to the redeveloper who, by signing
the checks, gets the right to be the final arbiter. As the developer,
you will be cussed roundly no matter what happens, by all concerned.

The General Contractor Problem
--Who Will Be the Contractor?

Of course, there is the possibility that a special joint
venture may be set up between the redeveloper and the local
general contractor. This kind of team work permits on-the-spot
supervision by a local man, who may have more political know-how
and contacts than you do. The local man's prestige and an understanding of local conditions, public relations, union organization,
etc. can be invaluable.

Presumably, you, as the out-of-towner, lend the specialized
Urban Renewal understanding, better financial connections, and
the specialized staff necessary to do the FHA, Urban Renewal and
tax processing.

If you are planning to use FHA financing and if you hope to
get the 10% sponsor's profit and risk allowance, there must be
"an identity of interest" between you as redeveloper, mortgagor
and the contractor. Most redevelopers would not (and could not)
finance an Urban Renewal project under §220 without the benefit
of that 10% sponsor's profit and risk allowance. It would be a
disaster to discover, at the end of the job, that because of an
inadvertent mistake in paper work you had failed to demonstrate
the necessary "identity of interest," to collect your 10% allowance.

You see, the FHA is willing to pay 10% sponsor's fee, but it
does not want to pay that 10% fee to a man who simply does the
packaging, and then pay another 10% fee by having it buried in the
costs, to the man who is really the general contractor.

As a result, most developers (who may have no building
skills at all) form joint ventures with contractors so that there
can be the required "identity of interest" between the sponsor and
the contractor. Working out these joint venture agreements is a
delicate field, but a most important one. You should recognize the
problems in the game to make absolutely certain that you comply
with all of the FHA regulations to get your 10%. In over-simplified
form, the FHA insists that before you qualify for the 10% sponsor's

profit and risk allowance, you must show that "less than 50% of the construction is subcontracted with one or more subcontractors, and less than 75% with three or less subcontractors."

Bonding Requirements

If the job is going to be FHA financed, a payment and performance bond will be required. Note, what is required is a payment and performance bond, not a completion bond.

If the LPA and the FHA both want a payment and performance bond, and you plan in advance, it may be possible to get both the LPA and the FHA as joint obligees on a single bond, thus saving your credit lines for other bonds and cutting bonding premiums to the bone. The bonding cost, of course, if properly done, is a certifiable cost and may be recouped as part of the mortgage proceeds.

Coordination Problems

In our section dealing with LPA negotiations and site acquisitions, we suggested that you might want to do some site preparation before title passes to you under the purchase contract. Such work may be vital to your timing, as a result of weather conditions, or in order to tie your work together with that of the road builders or utility installers.

It is most important to double check whether work done prior to the issuance of an FHA mortgage commitment will be reimbursable under that commitment.

Failure to clear this problem with the FHA in advance may result in locking in more of your money than had been planned. If you work the matter out in advance, you may discover that although the FHA will not directly reimburse pre-commitment expenses, it may adjust land values for you so that you can accomplish the same result indirectly. There is more than one way to skin a cat.

Another Problem

Another coordinating idea is to have the contractor who does your site preparation also do the LPA's share of the site preparation, wherever this is possible. In some cases, if you are going to handle your own construction work, it may be desirable for you to become the low bidder on the LPA's work, even though a small financial loss is involved, just to make certain that a saving in time and coordination can be achieved.

We all know of multi-million dollar jobs, involving interest charges of hundreds of thousands of dollars a month, being held up by the failure to make a sewer connection in which the local municipality's sewer man couldn't care less, because of the small size of his end of the job.

Adjust Values

In some cases where it is not possible to get the FHA to recognize site preparation costs as part of the mortgage, it may be wise to modify the land acquisition agreement so that the site preparation can be done by the LPA and thus included in the land value. In such a situation, the FHA mortgage would reimburse you for the land cost as valued for the improvements which would include the cost of site preparation done by the LPA. Thus, no problem in financeability under the FHA mortgage would arise.

Landscaping

Landscaping work is particularly important. Urban Renewal plans have a tendency to require building on as little as 10% or 15% of the site, so that the remaining 85% will exude a park-like atmosphere. Such an atmosphere is rentable and the amenities supplied thereby may be of great assistance to you. Some of the problems that arise: Are those trees and benches going to be mortgageable? Who will pay for it, and where will the money come from? We don't know what the answers will be on your particular project, but you had better know them before you start committing yourself to do it.

Some Legal Problems

Your lawyer, while all this is going on, will be busily forming such specialized corporate entities as "limited profit corporations," joint ventures, sub-chapter S corporations, etc. He will be making certain that the contracts between yourself and your subcontractors are so drawn that the sponsor's profit and risk allowance, which was discussed above, is safe. He will be sure that the contracts with your subs have appropriate protection in them to make certain that before the sub gets paid, his work passes not only the scrutiny of your architect and the local building department, but also the FHA, and that your subcontracts have the appropriate holdback and bonding requirements.

As mentioned above, your lawyer will also want to modify any contract between yourself and the architect to make certain that the architect's payment schedule ties together with the FHA's requirements, and that the architect will have the appropriate independence required by FHA regulations.

If you are going to have a number of separate FHA projects and mortgages, your lawyer will want to divide each job so that separate contracts and bonds can be gotten and that the architectural contracts, corporate entities, title policies and insurance clauses are all demarked, entity by entity and commitment by commitment. Otherwise the paper work will get hopelessly fouled up at the last minute and hold back the drawing of a check just at the moment you need it.

Timing

In chopping up a large job into a number of smaller ones, you achieve certain timing advantages. Since it will take longer to rent 3,000 apartments than 1,000 apartments, it may make very good sense to chop a large project up into three separate units, with three separate mortgages and three separate commitments.

FHA regulations adjust architectural fees, builder's risk and overhead allowances to the size of the job, so that you should be certain in advance that when you subdivide a large job into several smaller ones, the fees called for in each such separate project will ultimately be approved by the FHA. If they will not be, at least you will know in advance, and you can advise your professional team so that they are not disappointed in their share. On the other hand, if you are going to make up the difference between their standard fees and the FHA allowance fees, it is wise to know that in advance, too.

Assuming Liability for Omissions

If possible, the redeveloper should get the general contractor or builder to carefully review all the architectural plans and specifications in advance, so that the general contractors or the appropriate subs can assume liability for any increased costs which may come out of architectural omissions. If the contractors won't take the responsibility, will the architect? Remember, unless you buck the responsibility to somebody, it is you, the redeveloper, who will have to pay for someone's omission.

Foundation work is most important. Shall you insist that the foundation contractor do the requisite boring and subsoil analysis in advance, so he can assume the responsibility therefor? Will you be able to get him to do so? If not, who will be responsible?

Since, as we mentioned above, payment and performance bonds are required, they should be planned for as far in advance as possible, and subcontractors should understand their own problems thereunder. If there is going to be shopping around for an acceptable bonding company (for a bonding company which will accept the collateral you are going to offer, or for one which will issue your bond with no collateral), it is wise to know that as early as possible. The names of all of the interested parties should be endorsed on the bond at the beginning, to avoid the requirement of additional premium payments for adding additional parties later on. The bonds should be broken down so that each mortgageable parcel will have its own bond and its own multiple parties.

Construction Loans

At the same time you are hunting down your permanent FHA commitment, you should decide where your construction financing will come from. If you are dealing with § 220 or § 221(d)(3) projects, final F. N. M. A. commitments or permanent lending commitments are going to be indispensable to getting construction financing. Indeed, such construction commitments must generally tie Fanny Mae or the conventional lender to take over the construction loan on a certain date, at the expiration of the period allowed for both building and renting. Construction lenders, in most cases, want to know when they are going to be able to get out from the temporary construction loan. Without such assurance, they may be unwilling to make such a loan. Furthermore, the availability of construction loan funds will depend upon the condition of the money market in general. If an FHA insured construction loan is contemplated, it is most important that the contractor and subcontractors tie their payment schedules together with the FHA's commitment.

Recovering Construction Interest

Under the cost certification program, the construction loan interest and other carrying charges (including taxes) should be recoverable. A practical problem arises as to when the construction period stops and the operations of the completed building begin.

In other words, what portion of the construction taxes and what portion of construction loan interest is going to be recovered via the FHA mortgage, and what portion is going to be charged to operations of the structure which should be paid for by the tenants and recovered in the form of rental income. Obviously, the more interest and taxes you are able to charge off to construction, the higher your mortgage will be and the more money there will be left over for you as investor-builder. If you take a realistic approach to the length of time it will take you to complete and to rent up, you will find the FHA reasonably cooperative. While the operating expenses of the permanent building cannot be recouped under the construction loan mortgage, the FHA recognizes that in many cases it takes as long as 24 months to complete the job and its rental, and the FHA may very well permit you to write off 24 or more months of construction interest as a certifiable cost under the mortgage.

Cost Certification in General

§ 227, the cost certification section, runs through all of the multi-family housing programs in one form or another. § 227 is the result of the old § 608 windfall scandals. No longer is it possible for the builder-sponsor to share in the architect's fees. The amount shown as the architect's fee in form 2013 must actually be disbursed to the architect. Similarly, legal and organizational expenses must be disbursed or they cannot be recouped. While the amounts allowable as architectural and legal fees vary from office to office, you can find out what they will be on your size project by talking to the local office of the FHA.

that no land profit is possible. You should check out your own problem in your local FHA office. Theoretically, there is no reason why a land profit should not be permitted, since FHA does not require cost certification on land purchases, but is issuing mortgage insurance on the "fair market value" of land in question. Thus, if you buy a piece of land, hold it for some time, re-zone it, and find that it has increased in value, why should you not get a larger mortgage? Or, conversely, why should your mortgage be smaller than your neighbor's, next door, who bought his land later on and had none of that heartache of re-zoning to go through and thus paid top dollar for his land?

Whatever the facts are, make sure you know the rules of the ball game on your deal, and know whether you are going to get a land profit or not in your insurance commitment. Do not ignore the possibility of making that land profit just because it's tough to get. Explore it thoroughly and make sure whether or not it is available. Conceivably, it could be more important than all the other benefits put together.

Time Lag, Construction Costs and Change Orders

This entire book is dedicated to cutting time lag and pro-cessing time. The risk of that time lag can be disastrous in a rising construction cost market where you face a fixed mortgage commitment and rising costs. Even falling construction costs are not particularly helpful to FHA mortgagors, because of the cost certification program.

It is true that in a falling construction market you may be able to get a better job built (with more amenities) by getting the FHA to approve quite a number of change orders during the construction. This may help you do work that makes the project either more maintenance free or more rentable, but you cannot count on these changes.

It is most important to note that, if there is a change in cost on a particular item between the time the FHA gave you your final commitment and the time you actually make the payment to your subcontractor, the risk of that changed cost is yours, unless you get the FHA to approve it in advance.

However, if you, as the sponsor, bargain with your architect or lawyer for lower fees, you will not be able to keep any portion of the excess for yourself.

There is, in addition to the sponsor's profit and risk allowance, an allowance for builder's general overhead which you may include as a cost of the job, if you meet the other FHA requirements. However, you are going to find it pretty hard to run a building organization on less than the overhead allowance permitted by the FHA, as there is little opportunity for profit there.

Land Profits

Can you make a land profit on the land you purchase, and put it into the project? In other words, if you buy land for $100,000, can you get an FHA mortgage of $150,000 on it, assuming the FHA finds that the value of the land is actually $150,000 for mortgage purposes? •

What if you have purchased a piece of land, had it re-zoned, held it for a while during processing and otherwise, and found that you could make an honest profit selling the land off to a third party without building on it? For a while, such land profits in mortgaging were readily permitted by the FHA and they became particularly attractive in the § 221(d)(3) program where builder-developers put together co-ops which were sold to non-profit sponsors. The builders collected their builder's fees and added to them a good land profit.

A Change of Policy

Recently, and unofficially, the FHA has, by using "better" appraisal practices, tried to squeeze out land profits from the § 221(d)(3) program. Another pressure on land profits comes from municipal authorities who, in cases where they give tax abatement, have felt it unfair to give tax abatement to a builder who made a profit on selling his land, even though the builder was compelled to pass along the tax abatement to the tenants.

Nevertheless, since a mark-up on the land between the purchase date and the final mortgage date is an attractive bonus to a builder in a particular project, you should not take it for granted

Don't count on it. If you intend to change specifications as
a result of facts found after you begin constructing the job, think
through in advance and discuss with your architect who will pay
for those changes. If it is going to be the FHA mortgage, make
certain that you get it in writing in advance.

Room Mortgage Limits

When you come to examine the program-by-program analyses
in the next chapter, you will see that most FHA programs contain
mortgage limitations over and above the debt service limitations
discussed elsewhere. These limitations are the so-called "bedroom
count" limitations. Thus, you will see that under § 220, in addition
to having a 90% loan limitation, elevator apartments have $15,000,
$18,000, $22,500 and $25,000 limitations on one-, two-, three-
and four-bedroom apartments, while walk-ups have $12,500,
$15,000, $18,500 and $21,000 limitations. Of course, these
limitations can be increased up to 45% in "high cost areas." But,
these are the limits your architect will check out with you and with
his building cost estimators before you get started. Room counts
are now on a "per bedroom" basis, and the old "crazy" room
counts, which forced builders to construct dining "L's" in order
to get a two-count room out of a living room, are no longer
pertinent.

Since FHA's architectural standards and room counts
change from time to time, you will rely on your FHA architect,
who will know pretty well what they are.

The Joint Venture Agreement

We have mentioned the need for joint ventures between the
developer and possibly a local general contractor. Those agreements should carefully spell out the responsibilities of each of the
joint venturers, how they will share profits, and what their respective shares of the final equity of the job will be.

The agreement should delineate their respective financial
duties and obligations, both as to amounts of money and as to
timing. The agreement will also state whether the venture will be
a partnership, a corporation, a sub-chapter S corporation or some
other entity. Dividing the portions of the job to be undertaken by

each of the participants is most important. Who will do the masonry work? Who will do the buying? If one is more qualified than the other, obviously that man should have the responsibility and should do the work. It is common for the local man to be in a better position to do some of the labor while the national man may be able to buy stoves, refrigerators, hardware, etc. at lower prices, because he has his own jobbing organization. It makes no difference who will do what, as long as you clearly spell it out in the agreements.

Importance of Change Orders

When the final FHA commitments come out, they include in them cost estimates by the FHA on the various items which will control at the time of cost certification. The best way to get FHA cost estimates amended, either up or down, is by formal submission of what is called a "change order." In other words, if costs go up or down because the nature of the work changes, and if the change is approved by virtue of an FHA change order, then it will be added to the FHA estimate and you will get either a plus or a minus when it comes to cost certification.

On the other hand, if you have extra costs because you failed to make proper computations as to what the costs would be, and if the FHA did not catch it at the time the commitment went out, you are in bad shape. Such extra costs would not be allowable as over-costs for cost certification, and you may get stuck with more money in the job than you anticipated.

The time to know about these changes is before the work is done and the money is spent—if it is at all possible. That is the reason we reiterate over and over again that it is necessary to have a capable FHA architect on your team, and to have your subs go over the specifications carefully before the work starts. Once the money is spent, you are in trouble unless you can get it in under the FHA mortgage.

Non-Residential Space

Now you can include (under most of the multi-family programs) a mortgage on some non-residential space which is provided for the convenience of the tenants. Most of the multi-family programs permit a small amount of non-residential space, but FHA is much stickier about including non-residential space under the below market rate, §221(d)(3) mortgages than it is under a §220.

All builders are delighted to get 40-year self-liquidating mortgages on space which can be rented out to stores. FHA is most unhappy about granting such mortgages under the §221(d)(3) program where the interest rate is 3%. They cannot see why they should make 3% money available to build stores which then compete with conventionally financed 6-1/2% and 7% stores.

Under §220 of the Urban Renewal program, which calls for stores as incidental to the multi-family housing, FHA has less choice and is more inclined to go along on your loan—but the stores must be incidental to the residential space and not vice versa.

Store Troubles

Under the other multi-family programs, such as §207, FHA has experienced situations where builders estimated so much non-residential income for so many stores that when the stores failed to rent up, the project fell apart even though the multi-family portions of the project succeeded. Now, FHA is chary. Other non-residential space might be tenant parking and garage space, especially where required by local zoning ordinances.

Title Ownership Problems and
Other Government Agency Relationships

One problem is: how should title be taken? In what entity's name? In other words, if you are an investor-owner, can you hold title under the program, in your own name as an individual? Can you own in a corporate name or a partnership name? Programs which permit only corporate ownership, in the name of especially formed limited dividend housing corporations, prevent you from using the tax losses which arise from depreciation for your stockholders.

The FHA, on the other hand, has made provision for non-corporate ownership of real estate. Instead of insisting on an FHA charter for the corporation, FHA now gets the same protection through specially designed regulatory agreements. The owners are protected from personal liability by way of an exculpatory clause.

103

Replacement Reserves

The FHA requires developers to set aside, in escrow with their lenders, replacement reserves each year, which are accumulated to replace equipment which wears out during the life of the mortgage. Thus, if a gas stove is estimated to have a useful life of 15 years and if that gas stove costs $90, the replacement reserve with respect to that stove will require that $6 per year be set aside for its replacement.

Similarly, reserves are set aside for other kitchen equipment, plumbing, heating systems, air conditioning equipment, roofing, floor tiles, etc. Such replacement reserves vary from building to building, depending on the type of construction and what is in it. As a rule of thumb, these reserves can ordinarily run 9% or 10% of the annual operating expenses, or 2% of the mortgage. Replacement reserves are calculated on FHA form 2419, and examining that form is helpful in telling you what the reserves can be used for, and what they cannot be used for. These funds are deposited with the mortgage lender, where they accumulate at interest and are withdrawn only with FHA permission. They build up rather rapidly, and occasionally the prospect of freeing the accumulated reserves alone can be good enough reason for re-financing the mortgage.

FHA tries to be liberal on permitting release of the funds, provided they go to improve the project. The FHA would rather have the money used up to improve the job than to have the project run down.

6% of 11% Under § 221(d)(3)

You should know that § 221(d)(3), which deals with limited profit mortgagors (investor-builders), limits the return you can make on these below-market interest rate projects. Under the statutory formula you should look forward to a 90% FHA loan. The formula envisions that you will have a 10% equity in the project, and your return is expressed as 6% of 11% of the mortgage amount. In other words, the return is calculated on the assumption that you will have no more than 10% equity in the project—the return is calculated as 1/9 of the amount of the mortgage, not on your actual investment.

In order to make your 6%, you cannot have more than 10% invested in the project—so that if your foot slips even a little bit, you will not make your return. On the other hand, since the FHA knows it has you boxed in, it is pretty careful in its commitment and is reasonably flexible. But once again, a word of warning: Check all out in advance, double-check everything, and then you will know your return and be able to keep your investment down to the required 10%.

Of course, if you are building for sale (rather than investment) to a non-profit sponsor such as a church, a labor union, etc., all you get is your builder's fee. You do not get the 10% profit and risk allowance; and you are not concerned with the return on the investment, for you have none.

Chapter VII

FHA PROCESSING, FORM BY FORM

Let us take a fast look at the FHA processing picture so that the details will mean more to us as we go along. You locate a piece of land on which you intend to build an FHA multi-family housing project. Or with the help of renting agents and architects, you estimate what the cost of the project would be and what the rental income might be.

A Warning about Forms and Processing Techniques

From time to time FHA revises its forms. You should, of course, have an up-to-date set of blanks in front of you as soon as you begin to consider FHA financing. By examining those blanks, you will begin to understand the practical aspects of some of the requirements of FHA's programs.

The forms which we have used in this chapter have been selected because they are typical of the kind of information FHA requires. Some of the forms we have used for illustrative purposes here are concededly out of date. Nonetheless, we have used them because they break up into nice compartments the various steps of

FHA processing, and for illustrative purposes they clarify the problem more readily than some of the more up-to-date combination forms would do. Thus, under FHA's new, accelerated multi-family procedures, FHA's form 2012 and 2013 have been combined into a new form 2013 Revised.

Nonetheless, most of the information we discuss under 2012 and 2013 is still required by FHA; but, for convenience, we have separated the discussion into two of the older forms. Similarly, it is important to note that some of the timetables set forth in this chapter may be dispensed with. Thus, at one time it took from six months to a year to process a 221(d)(3) application. Under accelerated multi-family procedures (discussed herein), it is possible to accelerate that processing to the point where it takes 30 days.

But note that there is nothing compelling you to take the accelerated multi-family procedure; many builders who are just getting started with FHA will probably prefer to go the slower route, paper by paper, so that they can see the inherent problems step by step.

On the other hand, professionals who have gone through FHA procedures a number of times and know what to anticipate and feel they can get along without the FHA's looking over their shoulders and whispering in their ears, would probably prefer the accelerated procedures, since they save as much as a year of processing time.

If you plan to move along quickly, you had better know exactly where you are going and what you will do when you get there. If you take the slower route, you will learn more, see more scenery, and learn to correct your own mistakes without a disaster. On the other hand, the longer processing time will be more expensive in terms of paper work, and your cost estimates may slip away from you while the processing goes on and on.

Each builder will make his own decision—whether he would rather travel quickly or slowly; whether he wants to move along on his own, taking upon himself most of the risks and keeping the benefits, or whether he wants detailed guidance (and supervision) from FHA.

DEPARTMENT OF HOUSING AND URBAN DEVELOPMENT
FEDERAL HOUSING ADMINISTRATION

Form Approved
Budget Bureau No. 63-R1061.1

REQUEST FOR PRE-APPLICATION ANALYSIS OF
MULTIFAMILY HOUSING PROPOSAL
SECTION OF HOUSING ACT_____

Proposed Construction ☐   Existing, Repair or Rehabilitation ☐

Sponsor   Project

Name: _____   Name: _____
Address: _____   Address: _____
Tel. No.: _____   Tel. No.: _____

SITE INFORMATION

Dimensions: _____ ft. by _____ or _____ acres
Owned By: _____ or optioned _____
Present Zoning _____ Easements _____

UTILITIES: Public   Community   Individual *(If other than public a brief description of proposed installation.)*
    Water   ☐   ☐   ☐
    Sewers   ☐   ☐   ☐

Unusual Site
Features: Cuts ☐ Fills ☐   Rock Formations ☐ Erosion ☐ Subsidence ☐
           Poor Drainage ☐ High Water Table ☐ Ret. Walls ☐ Unstable Soil ☐
           Other (Specify) ☐ None ☐

Purchase Price: Actual $ _____   Proposed $ _____   Estimated $ _____

PROJECT INFORMATION

Walk-up ☐

Type of Project: Elevator ☐ | Number Stories | Row Type ☐ Detached Dwellings ☐   Semi-Detached Dwellings ☐
Type Construction: _____
No. of Units: Eff. _____ 1 B.R. _____ 2 B.R. _____ 3 B.R. _____ Other _____ Total _____
Proposed Rents: Eff. _____ 1 B.R. _____ 2 B.R. _____ 3 B.R. _____ Other _____
Beds or Spaces
(If applicable): Number: _____   Charges: _____

EQUIPMENT AND SERVICES INCLUDED IN RENT:

EQUIPMENT   SERVICES

☐ Ranges (Gas or Electric)   ☐ Laundry Facilities   ☐ Water (Hot and Cold)   ☐ Janitor Service

☐ Refrigerators (Gas or Electric) ☐ Venetian Blinds   ☐ Gas   ☐ Air Conditioning

☐ Kitchen Exhaust Fan   ☐ Other (Specify)   ☐ Electricity   ☐ Ground Maintenance

☐ Attic Vent Fan   ☐ Space Heat   ☐ Other (Specify)

Garages, or
Parking Spaces: Number: _____   Charges: _____
Commercial, if any: _____   Est. Income: _____

Names of co-sponsors, if any _____

If repair or rehabilitation is contemplated, the following information is required in addition to all pertinent data above:
Acquisition Price of Property: Actual $ _____ Proposed $ _____ Estimated $ _____
Date Purchased: _____ Existing Indebtedness, if any: _____
Estimated Cost of Proposed Repair or Rehabilitation: _____

AGREEMENT

The undersigned agrees with the Federal Housing Administration that pursuant to the requirements of the FHA Regulations, (a) neither it nor anyone authorized to act for it will decline to sell, rent or otherwise make available any of the properties or housing in the multifamily project to a prospective purchaser or tenant because of his race, color, creed or national origin; (b) it will comply with state and local laws and ordinances prohibiting discrimination; and (c) failure or refusal to comply with the requirements of either (a) or (b) shall be a proper basis for the Commissioner ro reject requests for future business with which the sponsor is identified or to take any other corrective action he may deem necessary to carry out the requirements of the Regulations.

_____   _____
(Sponsor's Signature   *Date*
(SEE BACK OF THIS FORM FOR EXHIBITS TO BE SUBMITTED)

108

SUPPORTING EXHIBITS

The following exhibits must be submitted with FHA Form No. 2012:

1. A location map or sketch positively identifying the site.

2. A sketch plot plan indicating dimensions of the site.

      This exhibit may serve also as a location sketch if street intersections, distances, and compass points are shown.

3. Evidence of title to the land, option to purchase, or owner's authorization to inspect the site for the purpose requested.

4. Executed FHA Form No. 2010, Equal Employment Opportunity Certification.

5. Additional requirements for certain special programs:

   a. Section 221(d)(3) Below Market Interest Program:
      (1) All Mortgagors: Estimate of the mortgage amount required.
      (2) Nonprofit mortgagor: FHA Form No. 3433,
          Request for Preliminary Determination of Eligibility as Nonprofit
          Sponsor or Mortgagor.

   b. Section 231 Housing for the Elderly-Nonprofit Mortgagors:
      FHA Form No. 3433, Request for Preliminary Determination of Eligibility as Nonprofit
      Sponsor or Mortgagor.

   c. Section 232 Nursing Homes: FHA Form No. 2576, Certificate of Need-the certificate to be
      submitted direct to FHA by the appropriate State Agency.

INSTRUCTIONS FOR COMPLETION OF FHA FORM NO. 2013,

APPLICATION FOR PROJECT MORTGAGE INSURANCE

FHA procedures divide the process of filing an application for project mortgage insurance into two stages, the first being the "Preapplication" and the second the "Application" stage. Formal application, through an approved mortgage on Form 2013, with fee may be filed when preapplication analysis by FHA has been completed, and the Sponsor is invited to do so. There is no fee for preapplication analysis and the proposal may be made by the sponsor by filing FHA Form No. 2012, Request for Preapplication Analyst of Multifamily Housing Proposal, with the appropriate FHA field office.

FHA field will provide advice and assistance to potential sponsors in connection with the submission of an application. FHA requirements vary in certain respects depending on, among other things, such factors as the Section of the Act under which insurance is sought, the nature and purpose of sponsorship, the size and character of the proposed project, and the special purpose of the project, if any. It is, therefore, extremely difficult, if not impossible, to submit an application which will meet all of FHA's requirements unless such assistance has been obtained. For example, except in most unusual circumstances, consultation with FHA will be necessary in connection with the completion of Section C, (number and composition of units, etc.), Section F, (vacancy provision and fixed charges), Section G, (General Overhead, Builder's Profit, Financing Expenses, Architect's fees, Builder's and Sponsor's Profit and Risk), Section H, (Off-site Requirements and Working Capital) and Section M of Part I of the application. Accordingly, the following instructions assume that all necessary preapplication advice and assistance have been obtained.

In any instance in which the spaces provided herein are insufficient for a full and complete itemization or description, attach a supplementary schedule and list same under M of Part I.

PART I - MORTGAGOR'S APPLICATION

A. Two types of FHA commitment are available (a) Commitment for Insurance under which FHA insures advances of mortgage proceeds during construction, and (b) Commitment to Insure Upon Completion under which FHA insures total mortgage proceeds subsequent to completion. Indicate which is desired.

B.2 As "Type of Project", indicate whether detached, semi-detached, row, walk-up or elevator. If walk-up or elevator, show number of stories.

-   Compute the number of rooms strictly in accordance with the provisions of the applicable Addendum to FHA Form 2013.

B.3 Under "Construction" show whether frame, masonry, brick and whether non-fireproof, fire-proof, etc.

Under "Accessory Buildings or Space" list the number of offices; specify the particular types of stores or shops contemplated and clearly specify the purposes for which any other space is proposed to be used.

C. The improper preparation of the Estimate of Income will cause substantial delay in the processing of this application. It is mandatory that the "No. Rooms Per Family Unit" and the "Composition of Units" columns be in strict compliance with FHA requirements as set forth in the applicable Addendum to FHA Form 2013. If units are proposed which can not be precisely described in accordance therewith, the FHA Field Office must be consulted for a determination of allowable room count and a full description of the units must be attached and listed in Section M of this Part. Show ALL units, including Non-Revenue Producing Space and the rental value thereof.

Since the National Housing Act is intended to facilitate the construction of income producing housing projects designed primarily for residential purposes, the need for the construction of all space (except garage spaces not exceeding a ratio of one space to each rental unit) which produces "accessory income" must be fully explained. If the ratio of "Total accessory income" to the "total estimated gross project income" is 10% or less, the statement of the need for non-dwelling space need include only a brief description of the services or facilities for which the space is intended, a statement of the distance between the project and similar facilities elsewhere and the ability of those facilities to serve the needs of the tenants. However, if the ratio exceeds 10%, the justification must be more detailed and shall include all of the foregoing, together with a detailed statement as to why the project might not be successful without space, a statement of the exact facilities needed and why they are needed, an estimate of the proposed rentals and an estimate of the gross receipts necessary to create a demand for the space, an estimate of the amount of such gross income which will come from project tenants, and the sponsor's reasons for believing that the inclusion of such space and the use thereof will not adversely affect the character of the project or decrease the acceptability or desirability of the dwelling units.

D. In the spaces provided list any facilities or services which will be provided and which are considered to enhance rentability or increase income.

E. "Operating expenses" are to be estimated on the basis of local experience. Adequate provision for replacement of equipment is mandatory. Do not include under this title any amounts for Real Estate or Corporate Taxes, corporate expenses of officers salaries, since these are not considered to be costs of project operations.

F. The assumed rent loss as a result of vacancies (including collection losses) will depend on local conditions, but must not be less than the prescribed minimum for the locality.

Consultation with the local assessor should be had in connection with estimated taxes.

OTHER FIXED CHARGES: If amounts are entered in this space, a full explanation should be attached and listed in Section M of this part. If a leasehold is proposed, show separately the annual ground rents proposed.

G. Estimated Development Costs.

"Net demolition" is the expense of demolishing old improvements to the extent necessary to prepare for new work, including disposal and other charges, less returns from saleable scrap and value of materials to be reused. Include only net costs. If salvage exceeds cost, show amount under Item I, Resources.

"Builder's General Overhead" must be shown here and shall be limited to a reasonable allocation of estimated central office expense of the builder, exclusive of salaries of its officers, directors, or stockholders. Do not include in "Builder's Fee".

Consult the FHA field office for a determination of whether "Builder's Fee" or "Builders and Sponsors Profit and Risk" is applicable.

"Builder's Profit" if applicable, shall be based upon a percentage considered reasonable and customary in the area for works of the same cost and character but shall not include any reimbursement for overhead.

The fee for the quantity survey-cost estimate, including land improvement items, shall be limited to the amount actually paid and shall not exceed the amount customarily paid in the area for such services.

Interest shall include only the amount estimated to be necessary to cover charges by the mortgagee during the construction period.

Include real estate taxes during the construction period only.

Under "Insurance" include only an amount sufficient to cover premiums for adequate fire and extended coverage, Public Liability and other property insurance during the construction period.

Do not include any mortgage discount which may be required.

110

Under "Title and Recording Expense" include only the estimated actual cost of the title search and title insurance, surveys, tax stamps and other mortgage taxes and recording fees.

Legal expenses shall include only necessary fees to legal counsel for services in connection with the project and necessary expenses paid by counsel for the account of the mortgagor.

Organization expense shall include only reasonable expenses not otherwise classified and which are necessary for the creation of the mortgagor entity.

Builders and Sponsors Profit and Risk, if applicable, is in lieu of the Builder's Fee. If Builder's Fee is included in accordance with the instructions above, no amount shall be entered for this item. If this item is allowable, the amount shall not exceed 10% of the total of all preceeding items.

H. Total Estimated Requirements

WORKING CAPITAL: The minimum required working capital is specified in the FHA Regulations for the section of the National Housing Act under which this application is filed, and the amount to be shown shall not be less than the specified minimum. Working capital is not part of the mortgage security. It shall be deposited with the mortgagee or in a depository satisfactory to the mortgagee and under control of the mortgagee primarily for the purpose of meeting the cost of equipping and renting the project subsequent to the completion of construction of the entire project and, during construction, for allocation by the mortgagee to the accruals for taxes, mortgage insurance premiums, property insurance premiums and assessments required by the terms of the insured mortgage. Any balance not used for the above purposes would be available for return to the mortgagor upon completion of the project to the satisfaction of the Commissioner.

I. RESOURCES: List only items and amounts proposed to be invested in the project or provided for deposit. Any items under Other Equity such as Builder's Fees, etc., shall be fully explained. The total must equal or exceed Total Estimated Requirements.

In rehabilitation cases, salvage (the excess of proceeds of sold materials over demolition costs) may be claimed as "Other Equity". The amount set forth as "Land" shall consider land without buildings. The value of buildings to be rehabilitated shall be entered under "Other".

J. Information concerning land must be provided covering the total area (including areas to become "off-site") to be provided in connection with the development of the project.

K. Site cost is to be completed with respect to all areas owned by the mortgagor or proposed sponsors and to be included in the project.

L. The total column shall agree with the item "Payroll" in Section E.

M. List of Attachments

REQUIRED EXHIBITS: Items 1 through 5 of the required exhibits must be submitted in duplicate.

1. The legal description of the site or sites on which the project will be located must permit ready identification of the land areas involved.

2. If any part of the land is to be acquired by the sponsoring group, copies of a valid option shall be submitted.

3. Photographs shall be of sufficient size to afford clear views of the proposed site and the surrounding neighborhood. Each photograph shall be identified to make clear from what point it was taken and the direction of the view.

4. A map of the entire governmental jurisdiction shall be submitted and shall be marked to indicate the proposed site, schools, churches and shopping facilities, business districts, industrial, commercial and recreational centers, together with main traffic arteries and available means of transit to and from the site to such centers, and any other factors having an effect on the desirability of the site.

5. The zoning map must be accompanied by a copy of the Zoning Ordinance, if any. In the absence of zoning maps, the map of the jurisdiction must be marked to show the character of zoning, zoning restrictions on the proposed site and the immediate neighborhood with respect to height, coverage and permitted use. This must be accompanied by definite assurance that the proposed project will not violate existing zoning regulations or restrictions.

6. Personal financial and credit statement, FHA Form 2417, must be submitted by each sponsor who is investing a substantial portion of the cash or other equity required to complete the project.

7. Architectural exhibits must include sketches and Outline Specifications, FHA Form 2435.

8. A quantity survey and cost estimate of materials and equipment, including land improvement items prepared by a qualified person or firm must be submitted. For rehabilitation projects, the survey-estimate is required only for the construction involved in the rehabilitation. The survey-estimate shall be submitted in the form and detail required by the instructions contained in Section 27, Volume VII of the FHA Manual. These instructions may be obtained from FHA field offices. Although a required submission, the survey-estimate need not accompany the application but may be submitted upon request after the preliminary working drawings have been completed to a stage satisfactory to FHA and considered acceptable for processing for commitment.

Other Attachments may include such items as a topographical survey, if required by the FHA Field Office, any proposed ground lease or an outline of the proposed lease, soil reports, surveys, etc.

N. The certifications in this Section should be carefully considered prior to signing. If there is any doubt as to the provisions of the FHA Regulations or their import, clarification should be sought since this certification constitutes acknowledgment of notice of requirements which FHA may impose as prerequisities to insurance.

Form Approved
Budget Bureau No. 63-R676.5

FEDERAL HOUSING ADMINISTRATION

APPLICATION FOR PROJECT MORTGAGE INSURANCE

(TO BE SUBMITTED IN TRIPLICATE)

| (To be inserted by FHA) |
| NO. |

| Date |

PART I - MORTGAGOR'S APPLICATION

Name of Project

A. TO:_____ and the FEDERAL HOUSING COMMISSIONER.

The undersigned hereby applies for a loan in the principal amount of $_____ to be insured under the provisions of Section _____ of the National Housing Act, said loan to be secured by a first mortgage on the property hereinafter described.

Insurance of advances during construction ☐ is, ☐ is not desired.

B. LOCATION AND DESCRIPTION OF PROPERTY:

1.	Street Nos.	Street	Municipality	State

2.	Type of Project	No. of Units	No. of Rooms	Average Number of Rooms per Unit	Est. Average Monthly Rental Per Unit	Per Room
					$ Mo.	$ Mo.

3.	Construction	Accessory Buildings or Space

4. Names and Addresses of Sponsors *(If Corporation, Trust, etc., Identify Officers and Stockholders):*

_____

_____

_____

_____

_____

_____

_____

5. Name and Address of General Contractor *(If, known)*

6. Architect's Name and Address	7. Name and Address of Sponsors' Attorney

C. ESTIMATE OF INCOME

No. of Each Family Type Unit	Percent of Total Units	No. Rooms Per Family Unit	Composition of Units	Estimated Unit Rent Per Month	Total Monthly Rent for Each Unit Type	Total Annual Rent for Each Unit Type
	%			$	$	$
TOTAL ESTIMATED RENTALS FOR ALL FAMILY UNITS				$	$	
Garages or Parking Spaces				$	$	$
Stores						
Other *(Specify)*						
TOTAL ACCESSORY INCOME					$	$
TOTAL ESTIMATED GROSS PROJECT INCOME AT 100% OCCUPANCY					$	$

RATIO TOTAL ACCESSORY INCOME TO TOTAL ESTIMATED GROSS PROJECT INCOME_____ %

NON-REVENUE PRODUCING DWELLING SPACE

Type of Employee	No. Rms.	Composition of Unit	Location of Unit in Project

D. EQUIPMENT AND SERVICES INCLUDED IN RENT:

EQUIPMENT
☐ Ranges (Gas or Electric) ☐ Laundry Facilities

☐ Refrigerators (Gas or Electric) ☐ Venetian Blinds

☐ Kitchen Exhaust Fan ☐ Other (Specify)

☐ Attic Vent Fan _____

SERVICES
☐ Water (Hot and Cold) ☐ Janitor Service

☐ Gas ☐ Air Conditioning

☐ Electricity ☐ Ground Maintenance

☐ Space Heat ☐ Other (Specify)

E. ESTIMATE OF ANNUAL OPERATING EXPENSE:

ADMINISTRATIVE:
Advertising - $_____

Management - _____

OPERATING:
Elevator Power (If any) - - - - - - - - - - - - - - _____

Elevator Maintenance - Expense - - - - - - - - - _____

Air Conditioning - Expense - - - - - - - - - - - - _____

Fuel (Heating and Domestic Hot Water) - - - - _____

Janitor Supplies - - - - - - - - - - - - - - - - - - _____

Lighting and Miscellaneous Power - - - - - - - _____

Water - _____

Gas - _____

Garbage and Trash Removal - - - - - - - - - - - _____

Payroll (From Schedule L.) - - - - - - - - - - - - _____

MAINTENANCE:
Decorating - _____

Repairs - _____

Exterminating - _____

Insurance - _____

Ground Expense (Materials Only) - - - - - - - _____

Furniture and Furnishings - - - - - - - - - - - - _____

Other - _____

TOTAL $_____

REPLACEMENT RESERVE - - - - - - - - - - - _____

TOTAL OPERATING EXPENSE $_____

TOTAL OPERATING EXP. PER ROOM PER ANNUM $_____

F. PROJECTED ANNUAL OPERATING STATEMENT:

INCOME:
Estimated Income (From Schedule C) - - - - - $_____

Less Vacancies Assumed

_____% on Dwellings $_____

_____% on Garages $_____

_____% on Other Income $_____

Total Vacancy Deductions $_____

Gross Income Expectancy (Gross Eff. Income) $_____

OPERATING EXPENSE:
No. of Rooms _____ @ $_____

Per Room Per Annum - - - - - - - - - - - - - $_____

TAXES:
Real Estate - Estimated Assessed

Value $_____ @

$_____ Per $1000 $_____

Personal Property - Estimated Assessed

Value $_____ @

$_____ Per $1000 $_____

TOTAL TAXES $_____

TOTAL OPERATING EXPENSE AND TAXES $_____

CASH AVAILABLE FOR DEBT SERVICE $_____

ANNUAL FIXED CHARGES:
Int. (1st year) _____% $_____

Amortization _____% (1st yr.) _____

Mtg. Ins. (0.5%) _____

Other Fixed Charges _____

TOTAL ANNUAL FIXED CHARGES $_____

CASH AVAILABLE FOR INCOME TAXES, COR-
PORATE TAXES, DIVIDENDS OR SURPLUS $_____

G. ESTIMATED DEVELOPMENT COSTS:

LAND IMPROVEMENTS: (Within Property Lines)
New Utilities - - - - - - - - - $_____

Landscape Work - - - - - - - _____

Other - - - - - - - - - - - - - _____

TOTAL LAND IMPROVEMENTS $_____

CONSTRUCTION:
Dwellings - - - - - - - - - - - - $_____

Garages - - - - - - - - - - - - - _____

Stores - - - - - - - - - - - - - - _____

Other - - - - - - - - - - - - - - _____

Net Demolition - - - - - - - - _____

Bond Premium - - - - - - - - _____

TOTAL CONSTRUCTION $_____

FEES:
Builder's General Overhead —

$_____ @ _____% $_____

Builder's Profit

$_____ @ _____% _____

Architect's Fee

$_____ @ _____% _____

Fee: Quantity Survey-Cost estimate (incl. land improvement items)

$_____ @ _____%

TOTAL FEES $_____

TOTAL FOR ALL IMPROVEMENTS $_____

CARRYING CHARGES AND FINANCING:
Interest _____ Mos. @ _____% on

$_____ - - - - $_____

Taxes - - - - - - - - - - - - - _____

Insurance - - - - - - - - - - - _____

FHA Mtg. Ins. Prem. (0.5%) _____

FHA Exam. Fee (0.3%) _____

FHA Inspection Fee (0.5%) _____

Financing Expense (%) _____

Title and Recording - - - - _____

TOTAL CARRYING CHGS. & FIN. $_____

TOTAL FOR ALL IMPR., CARRYING CHGS., & FIN. $_____

LEGAL AND ORGANIZATION:
Legal - - - - - - - - - - - - - - $_____

Organization - - - - - - - - - - _____

TOTAL LEGAL & ORGANIZATION $_____

Builders and Sponsors Profit and Risk - - - $_____

TOTAL EST. DEVELOPMENT COST (EXCL. OF LAND) $_____

LAND: (Available Market Price)
_____ Sq. Ft. @ $_____ Per Sq. Ft. $_____

TOTAL ESTIMATED REPLACEMENT COST $_____

H. TOTAL ESTIMATED REQUIREMENTS:

DEVELOPMENT COSTS - - - - - - - - - - - - - - - $_____

LAND - PURCHASE PRICE - - - - - - - - - - - - _____

TOTAL $_____

LESS Mortgage Amount - - - - - - - - - - - - - - - $_____

EQUITY REQUIRED - - - - - - - - - - - - - - - - - $_____

ADD Off-Site Construction Cost - - - - - - - - - - _____

WORKING CAPITAL - - - - - - - - - - - - - - - - - _____

TOTAL EST. SETTLEMENT REQUIREMENTS $_____

FHA FORM NO. 2013 Rev. 4/64

I. RESOURCES:

1. LAND: *(Names and Addresses of Owners)* — — — — — — — *(Estimated Value)*

$ _____

2. OTHER EQUITY SOURCES:

$ _____

3. CASH FROM:

$ _____

TOTAL RESOURCES $ _____

J. INFORMATION CONCERNING LAND OR PROPERTY:

Parcel or Lot	Present Owner	Total Mortgage Now a Lien	Interest Due and Unpaid	Unpaid Taxes and Assessments	Assessed Valuation Date - - - - - - - - - - - -	Current Tax Rate
		$	$	$	$	$

K. SITE OR PROPERTY COST:

Parcel or Lot	Date Acquired	Purchase Price	Additional Costs Paid or Accrued	Total Cost	Relationship - Business, Personal, or Other, Between Seller and Sponsor
		$	$	$	

L. SCHEDULE OF PROPOSED TYPES OF EMPLOYEES AND COMPENSATION:

Number	Type of Position	Rental Value of Quarters	Salary	Payroll Taxes	Total
		$	$	$	$

FOR FHA USE-ONLY

FHA FORM NO. 2013 Rev. 4/64

M. ATTACHMENTS:

Check(✓)	REQUIRED EXHIBITS		OTHER (LIST)
1.	Legal Description of Property	9.	
2.	Options	10.	
3.	Photographs	11.	
4.	Map of City or County	12.	
5.	Zoning Map	13.	
6.	Personal Financial and Credit Statement	14.	
7.	Architectural Exhibits	15.	
8.	Quantity Survey-Cost Estimate (include Land Improve-	16.	
	ment items)	17.	

N. CERTIFICATION:

The undersigned, as the principal sponsor(s) of the proposed mortgagor, certify(ies) that he (they) is (are) familiar with the provisions of the regulations of the Federal Housing Commissioner under the above identified section of the National Housing Act and that to the best of his (their) knowledge and belief the mortgagor has complied, or will be able to comply, with all of the requirements thereof which are prerequisite to insurance of the mortgage under such Section.

It is hereby represented by the undersigned that to the best of his (their) knowledge and belief no information or data contained herein or in the exhibits or attachments listed herein are in any way false or incorrect and that they are truly descriptive of the project or property which is intended as the security for the proposed mortgage and that the proposed construction will not violate zoning ordinances or deed restrictions.

Date _____   Date _____

Attest _____   (Signed) _____
                                                              (Sponsor)

PART II - MORTGAGEE'S APPLICATION

TO: THE FEDERAL HOUSING COMMISSIONER:

Pursuant to the provisions of the Section of the National Housing Act identified in the Mortgagor's application and FHA Regulations applicable thereto, application is hereby made for the insurance of a mortgage covering property described in the above application of the Mortgagor. After examination of the application and the proposed security, the undersigned proposed mortgagee considers the project to be desirable and is interested in making the loan in the principal amount of
Dollars ($_____), which will bear interest at _____ percent (_____%), will require repayment of principal over a period of _____ months and, according to an amortization plan to be agreed upon. Insurance of advances during construction ☐ is, ☐ is not desired.

This application by the undersigned proposed Mortgagee is subject to your commitment, its own final action and the payment of its charges. It is understood that the financing expense in the amount of
Dollars ($_____) is subject to adjustment so that the total will not exceed _____ percent (_____%) of the amount of your commitment.

Herewith is check for
Dollars ($_____), which is in payment of the application fee required by said by said FHA Regulations.

(Signed) _____
                    (Proposed Mortgagee)

_____
                    (Address of Mortgagee)

_____
                    (Name and Title of Officer)

First Steps

Having decided you want to take the slow route, you visit the FHA office for a pre-application conference. You are given either old FHA form 2012 (a request for pre-application analysis of a multi-family housing project) or form 2013 Rev., which requests the same basic information. If you pick up only 2012, it is wise to pick up form 2013 at the same time; or 2013 Revised, the new combined form. Either way, you will ultimately need the information required by form 2013 Revised, which combines 2012 and 2013. But we will break the problem into two sections by discussing 2012 and 2013 separately.

As we mentioned before, by the time you go to the FHA office, you will have located a piece of land, you will have a rough idea of what the cost of the project will be, how many units can be built on it, and what the rental income and expenses might be. We assume you will have made a couple of preliminary visits to the FHA (called "pre-application conferences") and are ready for your feasibility conference. Remember, our first discussion is concerned with the older, slower, step-by-step method of processing, which has now been condensed somewhat in the accelerated multi-family procedures, which will be discussed secondly.

Feasibility

Now, assuming you have had your pre-application conferences and that you have sounded FHA out about the location and the size of the mortgage, etc., you are ready to submit the pre-application form 2012. In a short time you will receive from the FHA a determination that the site is acceptable and that there is a market for the proposed dwelling units at the stated rents—or else you will receive a letter from the FHA telling you that they do not think the project is feasible.

Special § 220 Rules

Of course, if you are dealing with an FHA § 220 mortgage in an Urban Renewal area, the preliminary ground work will already have been done before you walk into the office, and the FHA will have determined that there is a market for the project and that a mortgage loan can be made on it in a certain amount.

FHA coordinates its activities in the Urban Renewal field with the Renewal Assistance Agency, so that by the time an Urban Renewal Plan has been filed and found acceptable by the federal agencies, FHA should have made a finding that it will make a mortgage loan thereon.

Formal Application

If the pre-application analysis has been accepted, you are now ready to prepare a form 2013, or a formal application for mortgage insurance. That form, when finally submitted, will require a check representing FHA's investigation or application fee. Once FHA gets form 2013, it begins formal processing.

Form 2013 goes into greater detail on the income and expenses of the proposed project, the cost of construction, and the amount of the mortgage. Form 2013 tests the project for economic feasibility by matching the income flow to the debt service requirements. It makes sure that after allowing all ordinary expenses plus a vacancy allowance, there are enough funds available to pay off the mortgage in accordance with its terms over its life. Form 2013 also allows for an additional cushion to protect the property against foreclosure in the case of minor economic variations.

Detailed Plans

If FHA finds the project acceptable, it will make a finding showing the value of the land, the replacement cost of the project and the amount of the mortgage loan to be insured. If these are acceptable, the sponsor moves on to the last phase of pre-commitment processing by submitting final sets of plans, specifications, surveys and cost estimates. The FHA reviews those documents and polishes up its original estimates of the land value, replacement costs and mortgage amount, and ultimately issues a commitment (form 2432), addressed to the mortgage lender (bank or other lending institution) with a copy to the sponsor, committing itself to insure a mortgage on the property in a fixed amount, and calling for a fixed payment schedule.

FHA FORM NO. 2432
Revised 10/66

DEPARTMENT OF HOUSING AND URBAN DEVELOPMENT
FEDERAL HOUSING ADMINISTRATION

COMMITMENT FOR INSURANCE OF ADVANCES

(SECTIONS 207, 220, 221, 231, 232 and 810)

Project No. _____

To: _____   _____
    (Mortgagee)   *(Name of sponsor(s))*

_____   _____
(Street)   *(Address)*

_____   _____
(City and State)   *(Name of proposed Mortgagor)*

The Federal Housing Commissioner, acting herein on behalf of the Secretary of Housing and Urban Development, will endorse for insurance under the provisions of Section _____ of the National Housing Act, and the Regulations thereunder now in effect, a mortgage on the property located at:

_____

_____

_____

and consisting of approximately_____ square feet, in the amount of $ _____ , subject to compliance with the requirements of the Regulations, the terms and conditions set forth below, and the attached specific conditions, if any. This amount, however, is subject to reduction prior to final endorsement of the mortgage for insurance as provided in the Regulations.

1. The mortgage shall be payable in monthly installments in accordance with the payment provision checked and completed below:

    (a) ☐ __Combination Declining Annuity Plan__

The loan shall bear interest at the rate of _____ per cent per annum payable on the first day of each month on the outstanding balance of principal. The first payment to principal (commencement of amortization) shall be due on the first day of the_____ month following the month in which the mortgage is dated. The mortgage shall provide that the first payment to principal shall be in the amount of $ _____ . Thereafter, on the first day of each succeeding month until the_____ installment has been paid, an installment of principal shall be paid in an amount equal to_____ per cent of the principal payment which became due on the first day of the next preceding month. The_____ payment and, until the mortgage is paid in full, all succeeding payments shall be in an amount equal to_____ per cent of the last preceding payment. The maturity and final payment date shall be_____ years and _____ months following the due date of first payment to principal (commencement of amortization).

    (b) ☐ __Accelerating Curtail Declining Annuity Plan__

The loan shall bear interest at the rate of _____ per cent per annum payable on the first day of each month on the outstanding balance of principal. The first payment to principal (commencement of amortization) shall be due on the first day of the_____ month following the month in which the mortgage is dated. The mortgage shall provide that the first payment to principal shall be in the amount of $_____ . Thereafter, on the first day of each succeeding month until the entire indebtedness has been paid, an installment of principal shall be paid in an amount equal to_____ per cent of the principal payment which became due on the first day of the next preceding month. The maturity and final payment date shall be_____ years and_____ months following the due date of first payment to principal (commencement of amortization).

    (c) ☐ __Level Annuity Monthly Payment Plan__

The loan shall bear interest at the rate of _____ per cent per annum payable on the first day of each month on the outstanding balance of principal. The first payment to principal (commencement of amortization) shall be due on the first day of the_____ month following the month in which the mortgage is dated. The loan shall be payable on a level annuity basis by_____ monthly payments of principal and interest in the amount of $_____ . The maturity and final payment date shall be_____ years and _____ months following the due date of the first payment to principal (commencement of amortization).

    (d) ☐ __Level Annuity Monthly Payment Plan (Sec. 221 (d) (3) Below Market Interest Rate Mortgage)__

The loan shall bear interest at the rate of _____ per cent per annum payable on the first day of each month on the outstanding balance of principal up to and including the date of final endorsement of the secured note. Thereafter, the loan shall bear interest at the rate of _____ per cent per annum payable on the first day of each month on the outstanding balance of principal.

The first payment to principal (commencement of amortization) shall be due on the first day of the _____ month following the month in which the mortgage is dated. The loan shall be payable on a level annuity basis by _____ monthly payments of principal and interest in the amount of $_____ . The maturity and final payment date shall be _____ years and _____ months following the due date of the first payment to principal (commencement of amortization).

2. At least 15 days prior to the anticipated date for initial endorsement of the mortgage for insurance, two draft copies of each of the following documents and exhibits shall be submitted to the Commissioner. After review, the place and date of the initial closing will be designated, at which time the following documents and exhibits in final form shall be delivered to the Commissioner for approval:

(a) The mortgage including the note evidencing the debt secured.

(b) The Building Loan Agreement between the Mortgagee and the Mortgagor governing advances of the mortgage proceeds.

(c) The Construction Contract, if any, between the Mortgagor and the General Contractor whereby the project is to be built.

(d) The final "Drawings and Specifications" (and also Drawings and Specifications for off-site improvements) conforming with those approved for commitment processing and with the additional conditions (if any) hereinafter set forth, and including the "GENERAL CONDITIONS OF THE CONTRACT" in "the Standard Form, current edition of the American Institute of Architects," and FHA Supplementary General Conditions, identified by all parties to the transaction.

(e) Contractor's Certification of Labor Standards and Prevailing Wage Requirements.

(f) Agreement and certification executed by the Mortgagee and Mortgagor.

(g) Architect's Agreement (appropriate FHA form).

(h) Title evidence in conformity with the Regulations which shall show that title to the property on the date of initial endorsement of the mortgage for insurance is vested in the Mortgagor free of all encumbrances other than the mortgage, and free of all reservations of title (either junior or prior to said mortgage) except such as are specifically waived by the Commissioner. If such title evidence is in the form of a title insurance policy, it shall by its terms inure to the benefit of the Mortgagee and/or the Secretary of Housing and Urban Development, as interest may appear. Such title evidence must be accompanied by a survey of the property, together with the Surveyor's Certificate showing that there are no easements or encroachments upon the subject property except those acceptable to the Commissioner, which survey will be extended from time to time during construction to show that the improvements on the site have been erected solely upon the land covered by the mortgage and within the building restriction lines, if any, on said land and do not encroach upon or overhang any land not covered by the mortgage nor upon any easement or right-of-way. Evidence will be required to show that the premises are not zoned or restricted so as to prevent the construction of the improvements and must include building and other permits from legally constituted authorities having jurisdiction.

(i) Assurance of the completion of the project.

(j) Assurance that adequate sewer, water, gas, and electric facilities will be fully installed prior to completion of the project and that necessary public streets, sidewalks, and curbing outside the project site, if not yet constructed, will be fully completed within a reasonable time after completion of the project.

(k) The Mortgagee's Certificate itemizing the charges made by you in connection with the mortgage transaction and evidencing the collection by you or your nominee from the Mortgagor of the following sums to be applied to the following items:

(1) Deposit to meet cost of equipping and renting the project subsequent to completion of the entire project or units thereof, and to be applied to taxes, mortgage insurance premiums, property insurance premiums and assessments required by the terms of the mortgage accruing subsequent to initial endorsement of the mortgage for insurance, and not included in the proceeds of the mortgage, $_____ . (NOTE: For Section 232 Nursing Home projects this deposit is required only for accruals of taxes, mortgage insurance premiums, property insurance premiums and assessments.)

(2) Funds, if any, required over and above mortgage proceeds for completion of the project. . . . $_____ . This sum represents the difference between the Commissioner's estimate of the total cash required for carrying charges, financing, and for construction of the project, including Builder's (and/or Sponsor's) Profit and Risk allowance, if any,) and Architect's fees and the maximum amount of the mortgage agreed to be insured. These funds may be reduced by so much of the Profit and Risk allowance and fees, up to a maximum of $_____ , as the closing documents show are not to be paid in cash.

(3) Escrow deposit, if any, to cover off-site utilities and streets, $_____ .

(4) The Mortgagor shall establish to the Commissioner's satisfaction that, in addition to the proceeds of the insured mortgage, the Mortgagor has funds in the amount of $_____ or has made financial arrangements

acceptable to the Commissioner in order to meet the expenses of the project from the date of initial occupancy until_____ months after the date of final endorsement as the Commissioner estimates is necessary to establish a profitable operation. The funds shall be deposited with the Mortgagee or other depository acceptable to the Commissioner on or before the date of initial endorsement, and such funds shall be held in a special account under an agreement approved by the Commissioner. (NOTE: Subparagraph (4) applicable only to Sec. 232 Nursing Home projects.)

    (1) The Escrow Agreement providing for the deposits, if any, required by Item (k) (3) of this paragraph and covering off-site utilities and streets.

    (m) The Mortgagor's Certificate certifying to the priority of the mortgage and to other matters set forth therein.

    (n) The instrument under which the mortgagor entity is created, unless the mortgagor is an individual.

3. The Mortgagor must possess the powers necessary for operating the project and meeting all the requirements of the Secretary of Housing and Urban Development for insurance of the mortgage. At initial endorsement of the mortgage for insurance, there shall be filed with the Commissioner copies of all instruments or agreements necessary under the laws of the applicable jurisdiction to authorize the execution of the mortgage and the other closing documents, and a Regulatory Agreement or other instrument to permit the Commissioner's regulation of the mortgagor as to rents, charges, and methods of operation. Such instrument shall provide, among other things, for the establishment of a Reserve Fund for Replacements by payment of $_____ per annum to be accumulated monthly under control of the Mortgagee, commencing on the date of the first payment to principal as established in the insured mortgage unless a later date is agreed to by the Commissioner.

4. (a) Approval of advances in accordance with the Building Loan Agreement must be obtained on a form prescribed by the Commissioner prior to the date of each advance to be insured. A Contractor's Prevailing Wage Certificate will be filed with the request for approval of each advance which includes a payment for construction costs.

    (b) During the course of construction, the Commissioner and his representatives shall at all times have access to the property and the right to inspect the progress of construction, and an inspection fee in the amount of $_____ shall be paid upon the initial endorsement of the mortgage for insurance. The inspection of construction by a representative or representatives of the Commissioner shall be only for the benefit and protection of the Secretary of Housing and Urban Development.

    (c) Upon completion of the project in accordance with the Drawings and Specifications the mortgage will be finally endorsed for insurance to the extent of the advances of mortgage proceeds insured by the Secretary of Housing and Urban Development, acting by and through the Commissioner, subject to reduction as provided in the Regulations.

5. Any variation from the terms of this commitment, or any change in the Drawings and Specifications, or any change in the conditions upon which this commitment is based, arising after the date hereof, must be explained in writing or in a supplementary application signed by the Mortgagor and Mortgagee, if the latter is required by the Commissioner, and must be approved by the Commissioner prior to the initial endorsement of the mortgage or, if made subsequent to such endorsement, prior to the date on which the Commissioner is requested to approve any further advance for insurance, which approval may be subject to such conditions and qualifications as the Commissioner in his discretion may prescribe. In the event of any change in the Drawings and Specifications, or in the conditions above referred to, without such approval, the Commissioner reserves the right to refuse endorsement or to withhold approval of any advance pending compliance with the original Drawings and Specifications and with the original terms and conditions of this commitment.

6. (a) If under the laws of the jurisdiction in which the project is located, the chattels and personal property of the Mortgagor required in the operation of the project are not covered by and subject to the mortgage, the Mortgagee must require and receive from the Mortgagor upon final endorsement of the mortgage for insurance a chattel mortgage or such other security instrument as may be necessary covering such personal property and chattels.

    (b) The project shall be equipped and furnished for proper nursing home operation. Any chattel mortgage, conditional sale contract, security agreement, lease, lease-purchase agreement or other type of financing arrangement designed to acquire equipment and/or furnishings for the project (other than cash purchase) must be approved in writing by the Commissioner and the Mortgagee, prior to being executed. (NOTE: The foregoing sub-paragraph is applicable only to Section 232 Nursing Home Projects.)

7. Any change in the sponsorship upon which this commitment is predicated must be requested in writing by the Mortgagee on behalf of the proposed substitute sponsor(s), and such request must be approved in writing by the Commissioner. Any sponsor or principal (including the principals of the parent entity, if any, of such sponsor or principal), who is now or who may later become involved in this project by way of financial interest, employment or otherwise, and who has not filed a certificate with the Commissioner fully disclosing their previous participation in FHA multifamily housing programs, shall file such certificate on the form prescribed by the Commissioner and must be approved by the Commissioner.

8. All forms, certificates, documents and agreements called for by this commitment shall be upon forms approved or prescribed by the Commissioner and shall be completed, executed and filed in the number of copies and in such manner as he shall prescribe.

9. This commitment shall terminate_____ days from the date hereof unless renewed or extended by the Commissioner. Prior to any renewal or extension of this commitment, the Commissioner may, at his option, reexamine the commitment to determine whether it shall be extended in the same amount, or shall be reissued in a lesser amount.

10. This commitment is conditioned upon the payment of a commitment fee of $_____ upon its delivery to the Mortgagee. If said fee is not paid within thirty (30) days subsequent to the date of this commitment, it

shall become null and void, and no extension will be permitted. A request for reopening received within ninety (90) days after this commitment becomes null and void will require the payment of customary reopening fee and the commitment fee.

Your attention is directed to the Regulations covering the assignment or the transfer of the insured mortgage, in whole or in part, and the transfer of your rights, privileges, and obligations under the contract of mortgage insurance.

Special conditions, set forth below or attached herewith, and identified as additional numbered paragraphs, are made a part hereof.

Dated _____

SECRETARY OF HOUSING AND URBAN DEVELOPMENT

BY: FEDERAL HOUSING COMMISSIONER

By _____
Authorized Agent

Initial Closing (Your First Money)

The borrower is then ready to go to the initial closing, which is the first time the FHA has really gone on a hook (by endorsing the loan) and the first time the sponsor-developer has been given any money. The first advance of mortgage funds is usually made at the initial closing.

FHA Insured Construction Loans

Actual construction of the project commences in accordance with the approved plans and specifications. The FHA holds periodic inspections and, if the construction loan has been insured, authorizes disbursement by the construction lender in accordance with the payment schedule.

Final Closing

When the project is completed, the mortgagor and the builder satisfy FHA cost certification requirements by completing forms 3378 and 3378-A, and final closing of the loan is held.

Following a reasonable renting period, amortization of the mortgage commences and regular monthly payments are made over the life of the mortgage. Other regulatory and reporting forms are involved from year to year, giving FHA the benefit of your statistical experience and also enabling FHA to find out if its limited dividend, rent control and other regulations are being carried out.

Form 2012 (Pre-Application Analysis)

Now let us go over the process in greater detail. Form 2012 is your first written contact with FHA. It lists the proposed sponsor, describes the site and the present zoning, states the kind of project (i. e., walk-up, garden, elevator, etc.) and the type of construction (brick, masonry, frame, etc.), as well as the number of proposed units (five 1-bedroom, three 2-bedroom, seven 3-bedroom, etc.) and the proposed rents.

Also shown on form 2012 are the kind of equipment and services to be included in the rent, such as stoves, refrigerators, venetian blinds, etc. , and water, gas, electric, heat, maintenance, etc.

If there is to be any non-residential use of the mortgaged premises (garages, parking spaces, stores, coin laundries, etc.) those uses are to be shown also.

Form 2012 is accompanied by a map or sketch showing the dimensions of the site and its location. You must also show that you have title to the land, an option to purchase it, or at least the owner's authorization to inspect the site for the purposes of making a loan application. The sponsor will have to submit form 2010 (Equal Employment Opportunity Certification), and certain specialized information is required of the sponsor in some of the non-profit programs (such as § 221(d)(3)).

Form 3433 (Non-Profit Sponsors)

If your interest in the project is merely to do the job for a builder's fee and then turn ownership of it over to a non-profit sponsor or mortgagor, the non-profit sponsor, such as a church, religious institution, labor union, etc. , will have to fill out form 3433. Briefly, this form calls for information as to the name of the institution, the date it received its charter and a description of the laws of the state under which such charter was received, as well as the purpose for which the sponsoring group was formed (such as to carry on and operate a church or a labor union).

The motivation of the sponsoring group with respect to the proposed project will also have to be set forth (such as the organization's desire to provide low income housing to families who are in need of decent and sanitary housing and who cannot afford the regular commercial housing, etc.).

The function of form 3433 is to help FHA determine whether the non-profit sponsoring group has sufficient motivation to carry out the program and whether it has sufficient finances and staying power to remain with the project for 39 or more years. Does the non-profit sponsor have sufficient personnel to supply the strength of internal management necessary to run a job of this size.

INSTRUCTIONS RELATING TO REQUEST FOR PRELIMINARY DETERMINATION OF
ELIGIBILITY AS NONPROFIT SPONSOR OR MORTGAGOR

Sections 221 (d) (3) and 231 of the National Housing Act, as amended, provide 100% financing for nonprofit mortgagors. A nonprofit mortgagor is defined in FHA Regulations as follows:

> "The mortgagor shall be a corporation or association organized for purposes other than the making of a profit or gain for itself or persons identified therewith and which the Commissioner finds is in no manner controlled by nor under the direction of persons or firms seeking to derive profit or gain therefrom."

The purpose of this form is to obtain the information required to enable the FHA Commissioner to make a determination prior to issuance of a letter of feasibility and acceptance of an application, that the sponsor of a mortgagor and the mortgagor itself, if the mortgagor has been created, is truly nonprofit in accordance with the definition above. The purpose of the preliminary determination is to prevent, as far as possible, unnecessary outlay of funds for FHA fees, plans, etc., by a sponsor or proposed mortgagor, who may be found ineligible. If found ineligible, the application will not be accepted. If tentatively found eligible, sponsor, mortgagor and the parties supplying land and services, in accordance with the terms of the commitment to insure, will be required to formally certify as to motives and relationships prior to initial endorsement of the note for insurance. A determination as to eligibility will be made at that time.

Determination of nonprofit eligibility requires a knowledge of the motivation of the sponsor and mortgagor, relationship between the sponsor and mortgagor, and relationship between the mortgagor or sponsor and the various parties or firms concerned with the project and mortgage transaction. A relationship involving an identity of interest will be considered adverse unless it is one that in the judgment of the Commissioner is beneficial to the mortgagor corporation, the proposed project and the purposes of the legislation. For this reason, it is essential that there be a full disclosure of all relationships and of all facts pertaining to each relationship.

In addition to completing the form on the reverse side, an exhibit giving complete information for each of the items set forth below must be attached. Where arrangements have not been made, it must be so stated and information supplied as to what is contemplated.

  a. List of the officers and directors of the sponsoring group including names, addresses and title of positions.

  b. Relationship between sponsoring group and mortgagor (existing connections or proposed, if mortgagor has not been formed).

  c. Statement as to the source or sources from which the sponsor acquired its capital and acquires its income.

  d. Statement as to the extent and source of subsidy or cash to be made available to the mortgagor.

  e. Statement as to the ability of the sponsoring group to render the support set forth in "d" above.

  f. Detailed statement of the arrangements made or proposed for the following, listing the principals involved, the relationship between such principals and the sponsor and mortgagor, giving the terms of the arrangements and describing the circumstances surrounding each:

  (1) Land upon which the project is to be built,

  (2) Construction of the project, including the selection of the general contractor, subcontractors and architect,

  (3) Legal and organization services,

  (4) Financing of the project, and

  (5) Management of the project.

Form Approved
Budget Bureau No. 63-R1055

REQUEST FOR PRELIMINARY DETERMINATION OF ELIGIBILITY AS
NONPROFIT SPONSOR OR MORTGAGOR

Under Section 221 (d)(3) or 231 of the National Housing Act

TO: The Federal Housing Commissioner

c/o _____

_____

_____

_____
Name of Proposed Project

_____
Location

Section _____
(221(d)(3) or 231)

The instructions on the reverse side of this form have been read and are fully understood. A preliminary determination as to the eligibility of the proposed mortgagor as a nonprofit corporation or association is requested. In order to assist in the determination, the information set forth below and on the attached exhibit is supplied.

1. The _____ received its Charter on
(Name of Sponsoring Group)

_____ pursuant to _____ of the laws of the State of
(Date)   *(cite Statute)*

_____ .

2. Purpose for which the sponsoring group was formed (as stated in its Charter):

3. Motivation of the sponsoring group with respect to the proposed project:

To the best of my knowledge and belief, the foregoing information and that contained in the attached exhibit is true and correct.

_____
(Signature)

_____
(Date)

_____
(Title-Officer of Sponsoring Group)

Non-Profit Sponsors

The FHA has discovered that most of the non-profit sponsors have the motivation, but many lack the capabilities and the personnel required to carry on a project of this size. You cannot set up a dummy corporation, in the hope of qualifying it as a non-profit sponsor, so that you can make a builder's fee. You are wasting your time trying to do that. You are better off locating a bona fide organization and interesting them in the project, and making arrangements with them to do the building when, as and if the FHA financing is obtained.

Note that you will be receiving a builder's fee here—not a 10% sponsor's profit and risk allowance. The builder's fee is usually less than 10%; the sponsor's risk allowance is always 10%. You should find out what the amount of the builder's fee will be before you start. In that way, you will know exactly what to expect, and you will not be surprised later. Builder's fees are on a sliding scale, depending on the size of the project.

Form 2530
(Previous FHA Credit History)

Form 2530 will be required by the FHA, either at the form 2012 or at the form 2013 stage, before a commitment will be issued. It is intended to reveal to FHA the previous multi-family participation of the sponsor and its principals. Form 2530 is also intended to reveal any deals between the sponsor and any third party called a "packager" or "consultant." There is nothing wrong with paying reasonable and recognized fees to packagers and consultants, and form 2530 is not intended to discourage standard building fees.

However, form 2530 is intended to reveal both the prior credit history of the mortgage applicant (to determine to what extent he has been involved in prior FHA mortgage defaults) and the real owners of the mortgagor corporation. Furthermore, if you, as the packager, intended to set up your own "dummy" non-profit benevolent organization, with the intention of qualifying for a fat FHA loan and making a fat builder's fee, form 2530 is intended to reveal the real facts and to get your application thrown out at a pretty early stage of the game.

DEPARTMENT OF HOUSING AND URBAN DEVELOPMENT
FEDERAL HOUSING ADMINISTRATION

Form Approved
Budget Bureau No. 63-R1061.2

PREVIOUS MULTIFAMILY PARTICIPATION CERTIFICATE
(Submit Original and Three Copies to FHA Insuring Office)

> The purpose of this certificate is to provide FHA with a full disclosure of past multifamily experience of all principals involved in the proposal so that FHA may determine the feasibility of considering the proposal involving these principals. Any doubts concerning applicability should be resolved by a full disclosure of all previous participation.

FHA Insuring Office _____ Case Number _____

Proposed Project Name_____ Location _____

The undersigned request consideration of a multifamily housing or Title X land development proposal (identified above) to be financed with a mortgage insured under the National Housing Act. The undersigned, individually and collectively, represent that to the best of their information and belief they are the sole "PRINCIPALS" in the project and they have not had any "INTEREST", by way of financial interest, employment, or otherwise, in an FHA-insured multifamily or land development project, except as shown below. The undersigned agree that any change of the "PRINCIPALS" listed herein, or additions thereto, will be reported to FHA and they will inform and advise new "PRINCIPALS" of the requirement to file a similar certificate with the appropriate FHA insuring office.

DEFINITIONS

The term "PRINCIPALS" includes, but is not limited to, corporations, partnerships, joint ventures, general contractors, sponsors, "packagers," or "consultants". It also includes architects and attorneys who have any interest in the project other than the normal,"arms-length" fee arrangement for professional services to be rendered, other than as a "packager" or "consultant", and stockholders having more than 10% financial interest in the proposed project.

The terms "PACKAGERS" and "CONSULTANTS" mean a person or firm, including attorneys, engaged to furnish advisory services in connection with the financing, construction or operation of a multifamily project, including, but not limited to, the selection and negotiation of contracts with a general contractor, architect, attorney or managing agent, securing financing and meeting FHA requirements.

The term "INTEREST" is not limited to a financial interest in the sense of profits, dividends, fees, and legal guarantees, but also includes nonfinancial interests such as a pledge of support, not constituting a legal or financial obligation, given by a parent organization to its member groups or a pledge of other nonfinancial support designed to convince the FHA that a proposal will be feasible.

The term "DEFAULT" includes any FHA-insured mortgage transaction which is or has been in breach of a regulatory agreement or delinquent for failure to meet required mortgage payments or, which has resulted in assignment of a mortgage to the FHA, foreclosure of a mortgage or a deed in lieu of foreclosure.

The term "MORTGAGE RELIEF" includes any FHA insured mortgage transaction which involved a modification of the mortgage, forbearance agreement or other similar relief.

Previous Project Name & Location	FHA No.	Name of Principal	Type of Interest	Default	Mortgage Relief

(With respect to each listed project which resulted in "MORTGAGE RELIEF" or "DEFAULT," as identified above by an ASTERISK in the appropriate column, the interested principal must attach a signed statement explaining the relief or default. "PACKAGERS" and "CONSULTANTS" must attach a signed statement describing the services they have rendered or will render in the proposed transaction and stating their fee. They must also include a statement that they have not and will not receive any fee or other compensation, direct or indirect, from any party connected with the proposed project, except as reported.)

EMPLOYER IDENTIFICATION NUMBER
OR
SOCIAL SECURITY NUMBER

Date	Signature and interest in proposed project
Date	*Signature and interest in proposed project*
Date	*Signature and interest in proposed project*
Date	*Signature and interest in proposed project*
Date	*Signature and interest in proposed project*
Date	*Signature and interest in proposed project*

WARNING: Section 1010 of Title 18, U.S.C., "Federal Housing Administration transactions," provides: "Whoever, for the purpose of ... influencing in any way the action of such Administration ... makes, passes, utters, or publishes any statement, knowing the same to be false ... shall be fined not more than $5,000 or imprisoned not more than two years, or both."

212012-P

FHA-Wash., D. C.

Pre-Application Acceptance
or Rejection

If your pre-application conferences have been well planned, and if you have done all your homework, you should now get a pre-application acceptance. This will come through to you in letter form, generally called "form letter B." Again, if you have done your homework properly, you should not get a rejection. You should not have gone as far as form 2012 if your pre-application conferences indicated the project would not be acceptable. The purpose of face-to-face conferences is to avoid wasting your time as well as the FHA's. On the other hand, occasionally one gets a rejection, and by making modifications in the program, one can get a final acceptance.

What Your Form 2012 Reveals

In any event, assuming you have been accepted and that they will approve the construction of x number of units and that if you file a form 2013 (together with the necessary fee) within approximately 90 days of the date of the letter and if you comply with all the other FHA requirements, they will probably issue you a commitment to insure a loan.

The B form letter encloses form 2013 and tells you what should be submitted with it; and informs you that after they get form 2013, they will issue a feasibility letter setting forth the estimated value of the land, an estimate of the replacement costs of the improvements, and the tentative amount of the mortgage. If you have gotten this far, you are moving along.

Form 2013
(Your Loan Insurance Application)

This is the formal application for a project mortgage commitment. Form 2013 will begin to cost you some money. When it is submitted, you are going to need a filing fee based on the amount of your application. In addition, fulfilling form 2013's requirements is going to call for reasonably detailed architectural drawings and cost estimates plus a detailed break-down of income and expenses. Once again, as you start to fill out form 2013 and at the various stages before it is finally submitted with the fee, you and your team should be conferring with FHA people constantly so that you get "feedback."

You will want them to be telling you whether they agree with your estimates of income; whether your calculations of operating costs go along with theirs; whether your estimate of real estate taxes matches theirs; whether the kind of mortgage you want is the kind they will give, etc. There is no point in doing a lot of work only to get a rejection at the end.

Form 2013 must name the potential lender (a bank, insurance company, etc.), describe the location of proposed improvements and the type of project (six-story elevator; semi-fireproof; two-story garden-type or walk-up, etc.) as well as the number of rooms, the number of apartments and the estimated monthly rental per apartment and per room.

Some Form 2013 Details

The name of the sponsor must be set forth along with the name and address of the general contractor, if already selected. The architect's name and the attorney's name should also be set forth. You will be estimating your income by apartment types (i.e. $100 per month for the two-bedrooms; $125 for the three-bedrooms, etc.) and estimating any income from any non-residential portions of your space such as garages, parking spaces, stores, coin-operated laundries, milk machines, etc.

The Dilemma of Non-Residential Income

On non-residential income, you face a dilemma. If you estimate it on the high side, you may be making the project look rosier than it will actually be. This may increase the potential amount of your mortgage loan (assuming FHA buys your figures). But, to the extent you over-estimate your non-residential income, to the extent you make the job look fatter than it really is, you are going to cut down on the net return FHA is going to allow you on rental of the apartments so that your rental schedule will be cut somewhat.

Always bear in mind that you face two separate problems in your FHA loan: (1) To get as large a loan as possible. If you want a large loan, you must show a large income. (2) FHA is going to limit your return. If you have a large non-residential income, your residential income is going to be trimmed. Your permissible rental schedules are going to be lowered. You must balance these two demands and decide which is better.

Gross Income Calculations
on Form 2013

In any event, continuing along on form 2013, you will have reached the point where you have added your residential income to your non-residential income (called accessory rental income) and will come up with an estimated gross project income at 100% of occupancy. This will include the accessory commercial income. Presumably, you will have tested out your figures both on a local real estate rental man who knows the market and on the FHA to see that everybody agrees on the reasonableness of those rentals. Again, because of the limitations above, if you can make the project stand on its own two feet without using the accessory rental income, so much the better. It will make the job look better for mortgage purposes to the FHA and you may be permitted a larger rental schedule on the apartments.

Enough Income to Service Your Debt

Unfortunately, in most Urban Renewal projects the key problem is to demonstrate enough income to cover the debt service. Since you usually want as large a mortgage as you can get, you want as much available income as possible. Thus, you will usually pick up all the laundry room, milk and cigarette machine income you can possibly fit into the project and add them to the accessory rental income.

Estimating Operating Cost Figures

You will then to on to get estimates of the administrative costs of running the project including advertising, management, legal, auditing, etc. plus the various operating expenses listed in Schedule E and the replacement reserves previously discussed, to come up with a total operating expense for the entire project and an operating expense figure per room, per annum. These figures should also be checked against your own experience or the experience of knowledgeable management people and the FHA should be sounded out before form 2013 is finally submitted. The FHA has a wealth of statistical information available in this field compiled from other projects both in your own city and across the country. If there is going to be a big discrepancy between your figures and the FHA's, it is wise to find it out early in the game before submitting form 2013 with a big check, only to get a rejection.

Do Forms 2012 and 2013 Together

As a matter of fact, we urge clients to fill out form 2013 at the same time they are working on form 2012. We like to face up to the facts as early as possible in processing FHA material. What is the point in wasting time on half a dozen conferences if your own pencil shows you the project is not feasible the first time around!

There is much to be said for your doing form 2013 with the assistance of your management and renting people, and your cost estimators before you even try out form 2012. If you cannot make your job look good to yourself, what is the point in trying to sell it to the FHA?

Vacancy Allowances

However, going along on form 2013, you should now have gone through estimating the income and expenses, and you should be at the point on Schedule F which represents the projected operating statement.

You will start out with the estimated income which has been compiled on Schedule C (representing both the residential and non-residential income), and you will deduct a 7% vacancy allowance on the residential apartments and a realistic allowance on the other income. This will give you a gross income expectancy.

Real Estate Tax Estimates

From that, you will subtract the operating expenses estimated at Schedule E and the real estate taxes, to come up with a total operating expense and tax figure which includes the replacement reserves discussed above.

Subtracting that figure (total operating expenses and taxes) from the gross income expectancy will leave you the cash available for debt service and profit.

From that figure (the cash available for debt service and profit) you will deduct the amount required for debt service (interest and amortization on the mortgage) and be left with an amount for income taxes, corporate taxes, dividends and surplus.

The Key Figure on Form 2013

Keep those figures in mind; we are going to come back to them later. The cash available for debt service is the key limiting figure. That is the figure which must support the mortgage application you are going to make.

Going to Schedule D, you estimate the cost of the land and the land improvements (within property lines) to get the total cost of the improved land. Here, your attention once again is called to the fact that you may have to put some money into off-site improvements and now is the time to find out how much you are going to get back and how you will get it back. All you are called on to put in Schedule G are the land improvements within property lines. If you are going to do some work off-site, now is the time to find out about who is going to pay for it and how.

You will also estimate the cost of constructing the dwellings. You will add in any demolition costs, if necessary, and the amount of the bonding premiums, to come up with the total construction cost. You will add on a fee for builder's general overhead, a fee for the builder's profit, an architect's fee, and the fee for cost estimating, to come up with a total for all improvements.

Carrying Charges During Construction

You will add the carrying charges and financing costs during the construction period. Now it is important to be realistic in your estimate of the length of the construction period. If you estimate an unduly short period, you may not get a sufficiently

132

large loan to reimburse yourself for the expenses.

If you estimate an unduly long period, you may find FHA asking you to come up with a large letter of credit or bond deposit guaranteeing to FHA you will be able to meet the interest, amortization, carrying charges and taxes required during the rental period.

Legal and Organizational Expenses

Schedule G continues by adding in legal and organizational expenses (which vary, depending on the site of the project and the particular regional office you are dealing with). You can find out this information by a telephone call. You will now come up with the total estimate of development costs exclusive of land and you will add the land to it, at the estimated available market price. Whether you will have a land profit or not has been discussed before.

How Much Equity Will You Need?

Adding together, at Schedule G, the cost of improving the land, construction costs, builder's fees, the carrying charges during the period of construction, the legal and organizational expenses, the builder's and sponsor's profit and risk allowance (where applicable), and the land at market price, will give you a total estimated replacement cost.

Schedule H will compare the amount of the mortgage with the estimated replacement cost to come up with the equity required. This figure is intended to warn you in advance of how much cash you are going to need when the job is completed.

The Income Available for Debt
Service "Trap"

It is most important that you go back to Schedule F and examine again the cash available for debt service. If your mortgage is going to require 7+% on a constant basis for interest and amortization, your mortgage is going to be limited to approximately 14 times the cash available for debt service. If your mortgage requires 8+%, your mortgage cannot exceed 12+ times the cash available for debt service.

A Way Out on § 220

Under § 220, however, FHA wishes to encourage construction of Urban Renewal projects so that it may permit you to curtail amortization of the mortgage during the first several years while you are renting up. In other words, the effect of this curtailment is to require smaller mortgage amortization, permitting a larger debt service multiple so that you can get a larger mortgage—a mortgage sufficiently large to finance the job.

Of course, this curtailment or postponement of mortgage amortization catches up with you in the later years. You are still going to have to clean up the entire mortgage balance over 39+ years so that the curtailment is no gift. On the other hand, it may enable a tight project to squeak through with a larger mortgage.

Re-Working a Close Set of Figures

In any event, if the cash available for debt service does not seem sufficiently large, you are going to go over the figures again to see if you cannot get the income projection up, or the expense projection down.

Perhaps the project will support slightly higher rentals. These may give you a considerably higher mortgage. Perhaps the expenses can be cut. These, too, will give you higher mortgage.

Bear in mind that if 7%, 7-1/2% or 8% is going to cover interest and amortization, every additional dollar available for debt service will support from $12 to $13 more of mortgage loan.

You now begin to see why we spent time earlier on the problem of the non-residential rental income in the project. We pointed out that flexibility in the vending machine, laundry room and commercial rentals could be helpful. You begin to see why you must be ready to justify your own operating and maintenance expense figures, if they differ substantially from the FHA's, and why your own estimates of real estate taxes become very important.

Lastly, you may wish to argue with FHA about the 7% vacancy factor in your particular market, and you will be going over all of your figures with your own experts.

Form 2013 Requires Exhibits

Attached to form 2013 will be a legal description of the property, copies of your options and summaries of your purchase contract, photographs of the site, maps of the city or county locating the property and a zoning map showing the zoning. Also required (on occasion) are personal, financial and credit statements, architectural exhibits and "quantity survey cost estimates" and any proposed land improvement costs. The application must be counter-signed by a proposed mortgage lender and must be transmitted with a check for the application fee required by the appropriate FHA regulations.

Various Addenda to Form 2013
(Including Form 2435)

Annexed thereto will be an addendum to form 2013, setting forth a schedule of the allowable room counts for your multi-family housing and a form 2435 outlining the specifications for the construction work so that the FHA can test out the cost estimates. Form 2435 will detail such items as the kind of excavation and the number of feet thereof, the details as to the concrete walls and footings, the masonry work, the waterproofing, the floors and cement work, the rough carpentry, the finished wood flooring, etc. Form 2435 consists of 36 or 37 detailed specifications. It is prepared by your architect after consultation with you (or the proposed general contractor, if you are not a builder yourself).

Form 2419 (Replacement Reserves)

Internally, the FHA will be preparing its own form 2412, its cost estimate. FHA will show you this form, if your cost figures are substantially different from theirs. They will also be preparing form 2419 which breaks down the reserve for replacements, and this is a form you want to look at, also. Internally, FHA prepares a form 2264 which represents its own analysis of the income and its appraisal of the project. Again, you may want to compare these figures with your own (form 2013). Form 2264-A will be prepared by the FHA, comparing the various criteria and determining the maximum insurable amount of the mortgage. This document represents FHA's internal preparation of certain sections of form 2013 which you have submitted, and winds up with a

DEPARTMENT OF HOUSING AND URBAN DEVELOPMENT
FEDERAL HOUSING ADMINISTRATION

Form Approved
Budget Bureau No. 63-R028.7

OUTLINE SPECIFICATION

MULTIFAMILY HOUSING PROJECTS

Not To Be Used as a Contract Document

Sponsor _____ Project No. _____

Project Name _____ Architect_____

Location _____ Date_____

INSTRUCTIONS: Describe all materials and equipment to be used. Include no alternates or equivalents. Show extent of work and typical details on drawings. Attach additional sheets if necessary to completely describe the work. The FHA Cost Estimate will recognize quality products and materials in excess of acceptable minimums, when specified.

1. EXCAVATION:
   Type of Soil _____ ; Bearing Capacity_____

2. CONCRETE WALLS & FOOTINGS: Concrete mix and strength for exterior walls below and above grade, interior walls and partitions, piers, footings, columns and girders. Size, thickness and location on drawings. Note portions having reinforcing steel on drawings. Location, size and material of footing drain tile and where drained.

3. MASONRY: Material and thickness of exterior walls above and below grade, interior walls and partitions, fire walls, stair, hall and elevator enclosures, chimneys, incinerators, veneer, sills, copings, etc.

4. DAMPPROOFING AND WATER PROOFING: Materials and method of waterproofing walls and slabs below grade, location, thickness or number of plies. Type of permanent protection of waterproofing (parging) if used. Method of dampproofing above grade. Flashing materials if other than sheet metal. Spandrel waterproofing.

5. CONCRETE FLOORS AND CEMENT WORK: Structural system of concrete floors at basement, other floors and roof. Thickness of slabs and strength of concrete. Attached exterior concrete steps and porches. If more than one type of construction is used, list separately and state locations. Material and thickness of fill and base course. Note slab reinforcing steel on drawings.

6. ROUGH CARPENTRY: Size, spacing, grade and type of lumber to be used for floor, roof, exterior walls above grade and interior partition framing, Subfloor, sheathing, underlayment and exterior finish materials (wood siding, shingles, asbestos siding, etc.).

7. FINISHED WOOD FLOORING: Grade, material, thickness, width, finish and installation method.

_____
_____
_____
_____
_____

8. MISCELLANEOUS MILLWORK AND CARPENTRY: Grade and species for interior and exterior.

_____
_____
_____
_____
_____

9. WINDOWS, FRAMES AND GLAZING:
   Windows and Frames: Type and Material. Special construction features or protective treatment.

_____
_____

   Glazing: Thickness, strength and grade of glass and method of glazing.

_____
_____

   Metal Curtain Walls:

_____
_____

10. DOORS AND FRAMES:
    Exterior: Thickness, material and type at all locations.

_____
_____

    Interior: Thickness, material and type for public halls and stairs, apartments (entrance and interior), boiler rooms, fire doors and other locations. Fire rating where underwriter's label is required.

_____
_____
_____

11. STAIRS: Material of treads, risers, handrails, balustrades, etc.

    Main Stairs   _____
    Service Stairs _____
    Other   _____

12. MISCELLANEOUS IRON AND STRUCTURAL STEEL:
    Miscellaneous Iron: Material and size of items such as:

    Access Doors   _____   Incinerators _____
    Area Gratings   _____   Lintels _____
    Coal Chutes   _____   Fire Escapes _____
    Foundation Vents _____
    _____

    Structural Steel: Framing or structural system used.

_____
_____
_____
_____
_____

13. LATHING AND PLASTERING: Type plaster, number of coats, lathing and where various types are used. Drywall thickness and joint treatment. Interior partitions other than concrete, masonry or wood.

_____
_____

14. INSULATION:
    Thermal Insulation: Thickness and type of material. Method of installation.

    Exterior walls   _____
    Ceiling below Roof _____
    Roof   _____
    Slab Perimeter   _____
    Other   _____
    Sound Insulation: Treatment of partitions, floors or ceilings separating apartments and between apartments and public spaces.

_____
_____
_____

137

15. ROOFING: Roof covering materials and method of application, weight of shingles, number of felt plies, bitumen, etc.

_____
_____
_____

16. SHEET METAL: Material and weight or gauge for flashings, copings, gutters and downspouts, termite shields, roof ventilators, scuppers, etc.

_____
_____
_____

17. PAINTING: Type and number of coats

Exterior   Interior

Wood _____   Wood _____
Metal _____   Metal _____
Masonry _____   Walls & Ceilings _____
_____   Kitchen & Bath _____

18. FINISH HARDWARE: Material and finish of exterior and interior locksets, sliding and folding door hardware, window and cabinet hardware, door closers, door knockers, numbers, etc.

_____
_____
_____

19. TILE AND BATHROOM ACCESSORIES:
Floor and Wall Covering Materials: Thickness, grade, finish and wainscot height

LOCATION	MATERIAL	
	Floors	Walls
a. _____		
b. _____		
c. _____		
d. _____		
e. _____		

Bathroom Accessories: Material and Quantity

Attached _____
Recessed _____

20. LINOLEUM: Location, type and gauge, for all resilient flooring materials.

_____
_____
_____
_____

21. WEATHERSTRIPPING AND CAULKING: Material and type.
Weatherstripping:

Windows _____
Exterior Doors _____
Thresholds _____
Caulking: _____

22. REFRIGERATORS: Capacity for each type of living unit.

_____
_____

23. KITCHEN RANGES: Size for each type of living unit. Gas or electric.

_____
_____

24. KITCHEN CABINETS: Detail on drawings.

Wall Units: Material _____; Finish _____
Base Units: Material _____; Finish _____
Counter Top and Backsplash Material _____
Other cabinets and built-in storage units: _____
_____
_____

25. MEDICINE CABINETS: Material, size and type.

_____
_____

26. PLUMBING AND HOT WATER SUPPLY:
   Fixtures: Material, size, fittings, trim and color.

   Sink _____   Shower over tub _____
   Lavatory _____   Stall Shower _____
   Water Closet _____   Laundry Trays _____
   Bathtub _____   Other _____

   Piping: Material and type:

   Soil Lines _____   Gas Lines _____
   Waste Lines _____   Standpipes _____
   Vents _____   Interior Downspouts _____
   Water _____
   _____

   Valve Shutoff for Servicing _____
   _____

   Domestic Water Heating:
   Direct fired: Type, capacity and recovery rate.

   _____
   _____

   Indirect fired: Separate boiler or combined with space heating boiler. Storage and recovery capacity.

   _____
   _____

   Insulation: Type and thickness of insulation on water lines and water heating equipment.

   _____
   _____

27. HEATING:
   Kind of System: Hot water, steam, forced warm air, gravity warm air, etc.

   _____
   Fuel Used: _____
   Calculated Load: _____
   Heating _____ , Domestic Hot Water _____ , Total _____
   Equipment:
   Make and Model _____
   _____
   Input (per hr.): Coal (lbs.) _____ , oil (gals.) _____ , gas (Btuh) _____
   Output (Btuh) _____
   Distribution System: _____
   Insulation: Type and thickness of insulation on heating equipment and distribution system.

   _____
   Room Heating Units: Baseboard units, radiators, convectors, registers, etc.

   _____
   Space Heaters: Type, make, model, location and output of heating systems such as wall heaters, floor furnaces and unit heaters.

   _____
   Temperature Controls: Individual unit, zone, central, etc.

   _____
   VENTILATION: Location, capacity and purpose of ventilating fans.

   _____
   _____
   _____

   AIR CONDITIONING:
   Unitary Equipment: Self Contained or ''Package'' units.

   Calculated load: _____
   Equipment: Make, model, operating voltage and capacity in Btuh for each size serving individual rooms, apartment units or zone.

   _____
   _____
   _____

   Central System:

   Calculated load: _____
   Equipment: Make, model, capacity, etc., of compressor, condenser, cooling tower, water chillers, air handling equipment, and other components which make up the complete system.

   _____
   _____
   _____
   _____
   _____
   _____

28. **ELECTRIC WIRING:** Type of wiring and load centers, number of circuits per unit, individual unit metering or project metering, spare conduit for future load requirements, radio or TV antenna systems. Show receptacles, light outlets, switches, power outlets, telephone outlets, door bells, fire alarm systems, etc., on drawings.

_____
_____
_____
_____

29. **ELECTRIC FIXTURES:** Type for various locations.

_____
_____
_____
_____

30. **SHADES:** Type of shades, venetian blinds or other devices for privacy and control of natural light.

_____
_____

31. **SCREENS:** Type and material of mesh and frames.

_____
_____

32. **MISCELLANEOUS:**

Elevators: Attach letter from manufacturer, whose elevator installation is proposed, containing a brief comprehensive specification for the complete elevator installation, and the manufacturer's statement that the number of elevators proposed and the installation described will provide adequate service and adequate capacity for peak periods, appropriate to the class of project, and equal or better service than provided in competitive properties, and that manufacturer maintains an effective service organization in the project locality.

Equipment: Garbage disposal units, dishwashers, clothes washers and dryers, mail boxes, package receivers.

_____
_____
_____
_____

Demolition: Construction of structures to be demolished and materials to be reused.

_____
_____
_____

33. **UTILITIES ON-SITE:** Material for distribution system for all utilities. Other land improvements.

Water Supply: Fire hydrants, yard hydrants, lawn sprinkler systems, exterior drinking fountains.

_____
_____

Electric: Light standards for lighting grounds, streets, courts, etc. Underground or overhead service.

_____
_____

Gas: _____

Sanitary Sewerage: Treatment plants, pumping stations, manholes.

_____
_____

Storm Drainage: Culverts, pipes, manholes, catch basins, downspout connection (dry well, splash blocks, storm sewer).

_____
_____

Underground tunnels: Material, construction, waterproofing and drainage of tunnels or conduit. Materials and insulation for utilities within the structure.

_____
_____
_____

Site Preparation: Tree protection, surgery, wells, walls, topsoil stripping, clearing, and grubbing.

_____
_____

Curbs and Gutters: Type and material.

Pavement: Material and thickness of base and wearing surface for drives, parking areas, streets, alleys, courts, walks, drying yards and play areas. Steps, handrails, cheekwalls.

_____
_____
_____
_____

Equipment for Special Areas and Enclosures: Play equipment, benches, fences and retaining walls.

_____
_____
_____
_____

34. LANDSCAPING AND PLANTING ON-SITE
Finish Grading: Approximate existing depth and method of improving topsoil. Extent of finish grading.

_____
_____
_____

Lawns and planting: Type, size, quantity and location of lawn, ground cover and hedge material, trees, shrubs, etc.

_____
_____
_____

35. GARAGES: Construction of all garages and accessory buildings not covered above.

_____
_____
_____
_____
_____
_____

36. OFF-SITE IMPROVEMENTS: Roads, curbs, walks, utilities, storm sewers, planting, etc., required off-site to serve the project.

_____
_____
_____
_____
_____
_____
_____
_____
_____

Sponsor's Statement. -- All items of construction, equipment and finish, together with all incidentals, which are essential to the completion of the project will be provided whether or not specifically included in the exhibits and will be of a type, quality and capacity acceptable to the Federal Housing Administration and appropriate to the character of the project.

(Signed) _____
Sponsor

By _____
Architect

FEDERAL HOUSING ADMINISTRATION

Project Name _____ Project No. _____

I - BREAKDOWN OF RESERVE FOR REPLACEMENTS

ITEM	Estimated Total Replacement Cost Including Installation Cost	Less % For Salvage or Trade-in Allowance	Replacement Cost Less Salvage or Trade-in Allowance	Estimated Useful Life In Years	Number of Replacements (during Econ. Life)	Replacement Reserve During Econ. Life (d x f)
a	b	c	d	e	f	g
RANGES: Res. ☐ Electric ☐ Gas						
CENT'L. KIT. ☐ Gas ☐ Electric						
REFRIGERATORS: Res. ☐ Gas ☐ Electric						
CENT'L.KIT. ☐ Gas ☐ Electric						
PLUMBING: Fixtures & Fittings						
HEATING SYSTEM: Boiler or Furnace						
AIR CONDITIONING MECHANICAL EQUIPMENT						
VENTILATING FANS & BLOWERS						
ROOFING						
FLASHING, GUTTERS & DOWNSPOUTS						
RESILIENT TILE FLOORING						
CARPET						
DOOR & WINDOW SCREENS						
ELEVATORS						
OTHER						

Total of Column (g) ·· $ _____

Annual Reserve for Replacements (Total of Col. g ÷ ___ years Economic Life) .... $ _____

II - DECORATING, HEATING & COOLING DATA & ESTIMATED CONSTRUCTION PERIOD

1. Decorating and Painting: Estimates of total cost to redecorate and repaint entire property:
   Basis: ☐ Materials only,   ☐ Contract (labor and materials plus overhead and profit)
   a. INTERIOR OF DWELLINGS (Public and Tenant Space)   b. EXTERIOR OF DWELLINGS - GARAGES & ACCESSORY BUILDINGS

   Total for Public Space .... $ _____   Total for Dwellings .... $ _____
   Total for Tenant Space .... $ _____   Total for Garages & Accessory Bldgs..... $ _____
   Total for all Interior Work .... $ _____   Total for all Exterior Work........... $ _____

2. a. Heating data: Type of system _____ Heat loss Btuh or sq. ft. radiation _____ Fuel _____
   b. Cooling data: Type of system _____ Heat gain or tons of refrig. _____ Energy or Fuel _____

3. Estimated Construction Period _____ Months

	Approved		
Date _____ Architectural	Date Approved	Chief Architect	Deputy ☐
Date _____ Valuation	Date	Chief Valuator	Deputy ☐

maximum insurable mortgage. Again, you will want to reconcile any differences with your form 2013.

Getting Your Tentative Commitment

If all has gone well, the first stage of your pre-application processing has been completed, and you are well on your way toward the initial closing, at which time the FHA will endorse its guarantee to the construction loan and you will get your first funds. You will have received form letter C giving tentative estimates of the market value of the land, of the replacement cost of the project, and giving a tentative maximum mortgage amount. You will be asked to submit preliminary working drawings and you will be warned about cost certification, which will come.

You will be asked to follow up, by submitting preliminary working drawings and specifications for review by the FHA, to be followed shortly thereafter by detailed quantity surveys and cost estimates. These will culminate in your acquiring form 2432— a commitment for insurance of construction loan advances.

Form 2432 will state the mortgage limits, lay out the interest and amortization plan applicable, as well as the term of the mortgage, and set forth the documents and certifications to be delivered to the FHA at least 30 days prior to the initial closing, including the various certifications required by the FHA from the general contractor, subs, title insurance, etc., together with such additional conditions as are applicable to the particular project, including the amount of working capital to be escrowed at the closing.

The Initial Closing

The FHA's legal requirements for closing are set forth in various FHA forms, depending on the particular FHA section under which the project is going to be insured. Thus, form 3618UR would be used for a § 221(d)(3) below-market interest rate Urban Renewal project. It represents, more or less, a checklist of the items to be brought to the closing.

FHA FORM NO. 3618-UR
Rev. March 1964

FHA LEGAL REQUIREMENTS FOR CLOSING

*Section 221 (d)(3) (Below Market Interest Rate) Project Mortgages
(Except Cooperative Mortgagors)*

Project No.: _____

Project Name: _____

PART A - INSURANCE OF ADVANCES

Listed below are the required closing documents in cases of initial closings in Section 221(d)(3) (Below Market Interest Rate) project mortgage cases.

The Closing Attorney will obtain three copies of each of the listed documents: one for his personal file, one for the Washington Docket, and one for the Insuring Office File. These will be either Original ("Or"), Executed ("E"), Certified ("C"), or Conformed ("Cn"), as indicated below.

The titles used herein may not be in accord with the titles used in some of the jurisdictions, but it is believed that they will sufficiently identify the documents desired.

Instruments	Form
1. Assignment of Commitment, if any	1 E, 2 Cn
2. Corporate Charter (See Guide Form 1731 for Limited Dividend Mortgagor) (See Guide Form 1732 for Non-profit Mortgagor)	1 C, 2 Cn
3. Regulatory Agreement (1730 for Limited Dividend Mortgagor) (1733 for Non-profit and Public Mortgagor)	1 Or, 2 Cn
4. Deferred Note, if any (2223 for Limited Dividend Mortgagor) (3622 - A for Non-profit and Public Mortgagor)	3 Cn
5. Lease, if Mortgage is on leasehold	1 C, 2 Cn
6. Land Disposition Contract and Deed (Required only if project is in an urban renewal area)	1 C, 2 Cn
7. Title Policy	1 E, 2 Cn
8. Evidence of Zoning Compliance	3 Cn
9. Building Permits	3 Cn
10. Surveyor's Plat	3 Cn
11. Surveyor's Certificate (2457)	1 Or, 2 Cn
12. Below Market Interest Rate Secured Note (1734)	3 Cn
13. Mortgage (FHA State Form)	3 Cn
14. Building Loan Agreement (2441)	1 E, 2 Cn
15. Construction Contract - Lump Sum (2442) or Cost Plus (2442-A)	1 E, 2 Cn
16. Assurance of Completion:	
(A) Contract Bond - Dual Obligee (2452) or	1 E, 2 Cn
(B) Completion Assurance Agreement (2450)	1 E, 2 Cn
17. Owner - Architect Agreement (2719-A, or 2719-B, or 2719-C)	1 E, 2 Cn

18. Assurance of Completion of Off-Site Facilities:

    (A) Escrow Agreement for Off-Site Facilities (2446) With Schedule "A"   1 E, 2 Cn
        attached
               or
    (B) Off-Site Bond (2479)   1 E, 2 Cn

19. Assurance of Utility Services (Water, Electricity, Sewer, Gas, Heat)   1 E, 2 Cn

20. Trade Payment Breakdown (2536)   1 Or, 2 Cn

21. Mortgagee's Certificate (2434)   1 Or, 2 Cn

22. Mortgagor's Certificate (2433)   1 Or, 2 Cn

23. Mortgagor's Oath (2478-UR)   1 Or, 2 Cn

*24. Statement of General Contractor (2482-A)   1 Or, 2 Cn

*25. Contractor's Certification (2482) (Strike all but paragraph 6 for nonprofit   1 Or, 2 Cn
     and public mortgagors)

26. Mortgagor's Attorney's Opinion   1 Or, 2 Cn

*27. Agreement and Certification (3305 for Non-profit and Public Mortgagor)   1 Or, 2 Cn
                  (3306 for Limited Dividend Mortgagor)

*To have been filed with Director at least 30 days prior to initial closing

PART B - INSURANCE UPON COMPLETION

    Listed below are the required closing documents in cases of initial-final closings in Section 221(d)(3) (Below Market Interest Rate) project mortgage cases.

    Items 1 through 13 will be identical with items 1 through 13 of Insurance of Advances. The additional documents will be:

14. Construction Contract, if used   1 E, 2 Cn

15. Guarantee Against Latent Defects (Surety Bond or Cash Escrow)   1 E, 2 Cn

16. Escrow Deposit Agreement for Incomplete On-Site Improvements (2456)   1 E, 2 Cn
     With Schedule "A" attached

17. Assurance of Completion for Off-Site Facilities:

    (A) Escrow Agreement for Incomplete Off-Site Facilities (2446) With   1 E, 2 Cn
        Schedule "A" attached
               or
    (B) Off-Site Bond (2479)   1 E, 2 Cn

18. Assurance of Utility Services (Water, Electricity, Sewer, Gas, Heat)   1 E, 2 Cn

19. Request for Endorsement of Credit Instrument (2455-- 2403A to be   1 Or, 2 Cn
     attached in Limited Dividend Cases only)

**20. Statement of General Contractor (2482-A)   1 Or, 2 Cn

**21. Contractor's Certification (2482)   1 Or, 2 Cn
     (Strike all but paragraph 6 for nonprofit and public mortgagors)

22. Mortgagor's Oath (2478-UR)   1 Or, 2 Cn

23. Mortgagor's Attorney's Opinion   1 Or, 2 Cn

24. Chattel Mortgage, or Attorney's Opinion Chattel Mortgage not necessary   3 Cn

**25. Agreement and Certification (3305-A for Non-profit and Public Mortgagor)   1 Or, 2 Cn
                (3306-A for Limited Dividend Mortgagor)

**To have been filed with Director before start of construction

145

PART C - FINAL CLOSING IN CASES OF INSURANCE OF ADVANCES

In these cases, the documents required for initial closing have, of course, been obtained. There will, however, be required these additional documents at final closing.

Items 1 through 5 will only apply if an increase is involved.

1. The Increase Note .... 3 Cn

2. The Increase Mortgage .... 3 Cn

3. The Consolidation Agreement .... 3 Cn
   or
4. A new Note and Mortgage for the total .... 3 Cn

5. Mortgagor's Attorney's Opinion as to Increase .... 1 E, 2 Cn

6. Chattel Mortgage .... 3 Cn
   or
   Attorney's Opinion Chattel Mortgage not necessary .... 1 E, 2 Cn

7. Title Policy brought up to date .... 1 E, 2 Cn

8. Survey showing completed Project .... 3 Cn

9. Surveyor's Certificate (2457) .... 1 Or, 2 Cn

10. Assurance of completion for:

    (A) Incomplete Off-Site Facilities:
        (1) Escrow Deposit Agreement (2446) with Schedule "A" attached ... 1 E, 2 Cn
        or
        (2) Off-Site Bond (2479) .... 1 E, 2 Cn

    (B) Incomplete On-Site Facilities:
        Escrow Deposit Agreement (2456) with Schedule "A" attached ... 1 E, 2 Cn

11. Request for Final Endorsement of Credit Instrument (2023) ... 1 Or, 2 Cn

Name of Mortgagor: _____

Address of Mortgagor: _____

Name of Mortgagee: _____

Address of Mortgagee: _____

There would be no point in this work in going through the requirements of each and every one of the required closing documents, except to state that if you have never had an FHA closing before, a "dry run" at the FHA offices should take place sufficiently in advance of the actual closing so that any papers which do not meet the exacting standards of the various legal and underwriting personnel can be revised in time to take down the money as planned.

Why a "Dry Run" Is Vital to Your Closing

The more time spent by your attorney in advance of the actual closing in going over his papers with the various interested parties, the less time the closing will take and the more certain you are to receive the money. Twenty-five separate technical legal documents are listed on form 3618UR and all these represent several hundred pages of documentation containing tens of thousands of technical words, any one of which can cost you a fortune if you are not warned about it in advance.

It would be well for you, your architect, your attorney and your accountant to review the necessary forms at the time the commitment comes through (long before the actual closing) so that each of you will know what he must do in order to insure the procuring of the necessary documents and to avoid any loose nuts and bolts which may get into the gears of the money-issuing machinery. Every FHA-experienced attorney prepares an agenda, a checklist, and follows it up to make sure there will be no "foul up" at the closing.

Chapter VIII

KEY TERMS OF THE VARIOUS FHA LOAN PROGRAMS

It will be the purpose of this section to digest the FHA insured loan programs currently available in the Urban Renewal and multi-family housing fields. Of course, the standard § 207 and § 213 programs are also available, but there is nothing unique about them as they apply to Urban Renewal. They are the standard FHA programs for management-owned multi-family apartments involving 90% loans at full market interest rates for investor-owned multi-family construction in § 207 and 97% loans for co-ops ("tenant-owned").

Those two loan programs (§ 207 and § 213) are available in non-Urban Renewal areas as well as in Urban Renewal areas.

When we come to Urban Renewal areas, however, we have three major programs of interest: First, there is the § 220 one-family home program at standard interest rates. Second, there is the § 220 multi-family home program which is a standard interest rate program. Finally, there is the § 221(d)(3) program which is a 3% below-market interest program for low income families.

In these three areas—§220 single-family, §220 multi-family and §221(d)(3)—lies the bulk of Urban Renewal activity. The following pages, in outline form, digest each of these programs, item by item. Of course, you will want to check out with your local FHA office and your attorney the current regulations on these projects in your particular area. Administrative changes are going on, on a day-to-day basis, region by region.

Check These Out Locally

From here on in you will be receiving construction loan advances, from time to time, with your architect coordinating his work with the FHA's architectural staff so that certification may be made to the lender and to the FHA. These certifications are pre-requisites to getting paid.

Except for the fact that there is an additional inspection at the FHA level, much of the construction loan advance procedures, once the FHA's preliminary paper work has been done, are so similar to standard construction lending that separate treatment is not warranted here.

Guide to Accelerated Multi-Family Procedures

Because of complaints to the effect that FHA processing on many programs took as long as a year or two, the FHA, the National Association of Home Builders, the National Association of Housing and Redevelopment Officials, and a number of other trade associations combined their thinking to set up a new method of speeding up multi-family processing. Called "AMP" by FHA, the "Accelerated Multi-family Processing" technique offers knowledgeable builders an opportunity to get a firm FHA commitment in as little as thirty days. You pay for the speed-up in processing, of course, since you are then locked into that commitment, whether it turns out to be to your benefit or not. You had better be sure in advance that you understand all the FHA regulations and design requirements by the time you take down the insurance commitment, because if you start to build anticipating something that the FHA does not permit, you could have substantial troubles. Nonetheless, we are going to devote the rest of this section to explaining how AMP works, by abstracting from FHA's guide on the subject, so that builders who desire to take down the commitment in as little as 30 days can see how it is done.

I. Introduction to AMP

(Note: The emphasis and parenthetical material has been supplied by your author—not by FHA)

The purpose of this guide is to provide basic information to prospective sponsors who are interested in developing multi-family projects under FHA programs. The guide introduces a new system, designed to drastically reduce processing time, called Accelerated Multi-family Processing (AMP). Under this procedure FHA is committed to processing a project, from the time of initial contact with a sponsor to construction of the project, as rapidly as possible, consistent with accuracy. Fundamental to this concept, insofar as the sponsor is concerned, are the following:

1. All key decisions concerning project feasibility, including the location, project size and type, rental rates, the construction budget, the land value, and the tentative mortgage amount, are made at the feasibility conference with the sponsor prior to any necessary expenditure on the sponsor's part. Project design and cost must generally conform to the project budget and cannot be exceeded.

2. FHA will adhere to a strict processing schedule using accelerated procedures involving all phases of its processing operations. These procedures will reduce action time from months to hours in many instances. The sponsor, for his part, will be expected to move forward with all possible speed. Mutually agreed upon target dates must be adhered to.

3. Under AMP procedures and stages are completely flexible, dependent upon the sponsor's needs. The knowledgeable sponsor with a complete set of exhibits for an otherwise acceptable proposal can have his project processed in a single stage leading directly to a firm commitment. The sponsor with only an idea in mind may be processed through all stages; i.e., feasibility, conditional commitment and final commitment (the slower, more certain route).

150

4. Wherever possible the AMP process permits assignment of an FHA design representative to work with the sponsor's architect in the design phase of the project. This procedure permits project design development without costly and time-consuming redesign to meet FHA criteria or objections to sponsor's architect submissions. (FHA's design people visit and work with your architect at his office).

To those sponsors who will be doing business with FHA for the first time, you will find a willing and capable staff anxious to assist you in every way to produce sorely needed housing as efficiently and expeditiously as possible. To those sponsors who have had previous experience with FHA's time-consuming old procedures, we invite you to a new and rewarding experience.

II. The Stages of Project Processing

Under the AMP program, which emphasizes flexible project processing procedures, the Multi-family Coordinator, who is the point of contact with the sponsor, will schedule project processing in either one, two or three stages.

Under single stage processing, the sponsor provides at the first submission all of his and FHA's requirements. The sponsor's complete case submission may be processed in one stage with the issuance of a firm commitment. Total elapsed time between the first contact and the FHA's issuance of the commitment would be approximately thirty days. (This requires a full set of final plans and specs on submission.)

Under multiple stage processing, the sponsor may be unable to satisfy all of his and the FHA's requirements in the first submission, but FHA considers the proposal to be generally acceptable. In this instance, the sponsor would be carried through two or three stages—the first leading to a feasibility letter, the second leading to a conditional commitment, and the third, to firm commitment.

The total AMP processing procedure is as follows:

1. The first contact between the sponsor and the FHA insuring office on the proposal.

2. Preparation of informal application form by sponsor outlining his proposal.
3. Preparation for the Feasibility Conference by both the sponsor and the local insuring office.
4. The Feasibility Conference and issuance of a Feasibility Letter.
5. Preparation of forms, exhibits and preliminary sketches and brief specifications by the sponsor and payment of application fee if conditional commitment is requested.
6. FHA processing of the sponsor's exhibits and issuance of a conditional commitment.
7. Complete architectural design of the project.
8. Sponsor's payment of application fee (unless already paid) and commitment fee, FHA review of contract drawings and documents, and FHA issuance of the firm commitment.
9. Initial endorsement of the original credit instrument, referred to as the initial closing.
10. Pre-Construction Conference.
11. Construction of the project.

Under AMP, FHA is committed to help the sponsor meet the existing market on time. Processing is rapid even when a sponsor goes through all the steps described above.

III. Information Required from the Sponsor at First Contact

At the first contact with the FHA office, whether by letter or in person, the sponsor should be prepared to give the Multifamily Coordinator all the information not marked with solid triangles on the application form (2013 Rev). This application form is used in all stages; as a sponsor's summary and preapplication in feasibility and conditional commitment stages and as the mortgagee's application in final commitment.

The required information is only necessary to identify and provide access to site, number of units, the expected income in terms of rents, a rough estimate as to costs, and a requested loan amount. However, any additional specific information the sponsor already has should be furnished as well. The sponsor should have a clear idea of the demand for housing of the type proposed in the area of his project, the extent of competition with which he will be confronted, the vacancy rates in similar apartments, and the prevailing rent levels in the neighborhood. He should also know the garage accommodations, equipment, and services included in the rentals of competing structures. Other essential information includes knowledge of whether his site location is acceptable to the type of tenants he wishes to attract to his project and whether zoning for his site is permissive for his proposed project. At this point it is also desirable that the sponsor have an indication of the total construction and land improvement costs for the proposed project. The FHA coordinator will have this information analyzed and, using data and information available in the insuring office, a determination will be made if the project is economically feasible in terms of site acceptability, number of units, rents, expenses, net income, land value, a project budget, cash requirements and a mortgage amount. A Feasibility Conference is then scheduled.

IV. Sponsor's Preparation for Feasibility Conference

Prior to the Feasibility Conference, and in addition to the information supplied at the first contact, the sponsor should provide the FHA office with any data or exhibits he may already have that will help to determine the project's economic feasibility. The sponsor, however, should not incur any expenses at this point for the development of any data which he does not already possess. Neither should an architect be hired, an engineer employed, nor expenses incurred until the general determinations of project eligibility have been made during the Feasibility Conference. However, if already selected, the architect should accompany the sponsor to the Feasibility Conference and should be made familiar with the FHA procedure as outlined in the "Ground Rules for the Sponsor's Architect."

The feasibility determination can be made without any drawings or sketches whatsoever. This can be done by setting specific budget limits for an economically feasible project and then designing the project to meet them. This approach has been found to produce superior results to one of trying to establish the feasibility of plans which are drawn without due consideration to the governing factors of economic workability.

V. The Feasibility Conference and Issuance of a Feasibility Letter

FHA will schedule a Feasibility Conference to discuss the economic feasibility of the proposed project. Economic feasibility refers to the capability of the project to produce sufficient income to pay the operating and fixed expenses, meet the mortgage requirements and leave a reasonable net return to the profit-motivated sponsor. The following will be discussed furing the Feasibility Conference:

1. Sponsorship

The financial capability, reputation, experience and ability of the sponsor will be analyzed to ascertain whether or not he has the capability to develop a successful project and the cash necessary to complete it, if any. Neither FHA nor the sponsor can afford to embark upon a project which is obviously risky because of the sponsor's lack of experience, ability, or required financial resources.

2. Marketability

The sponsor must be prepared to discuss the need for his project in the specific area as it relates to proposed rentals, composition, and unit sizes. Market data developed by the FHA insuring office will be made available to the sponsor.

3. Building and Site Plan Suitability

Although detailed drawings are neither required nor encouraged at this time, the general design concept will be discussed, including the number and placement of buildings on the site, the composition of apartment units (number of 1-bedroom, 2-bedroom, etc.), as well as the location and extent of parking and recreational facilities. In order to assure design excellence, a registered architect is required on all elevator projects and other projects with sixteen or more units. To successfully perform the design services on complex projects, he will be expected to consult with the engineers and planners of his choice.

4. Management Program

Management plays such an important role in the ultimate success of a project that a definite management program is required. The overall management program will be discussed with the sponsor, and points which will be covered will include the type of management contract proposed between the sponsor and his agent, standard lease forms, rental and collection policies, uniform system of accounts and financial reports required by FHA, the rendering of monthly statements to the owner, project maintenance and repair programs, among others. After construction, FHA management specialists will periodically review the management program with emphasis on both the financial and the physical condition of the project.

5. Determination of Feasibility

The final determination of project economic feasibility is made and agreement between the sponsor and FHA on the above matters is reached. If the sponsor's estimated project replacement cost and requested loan amount do not exceed by more than 2% the maximum cost and mortgage amount which can be supported by the project net income as initially calculated by FHA, the project can almost certainly be considered economically feasible. This feasibility may be achieved by (1) minor adjustments to rents, where Statute and Regulation permit such adjustments, or (2) by eliminating non-essential items from the plans and specifications, or (3) by a slight additional cash investment by the sponsor.

During the Feasibility Conference the Multifamily Coordinator will discuss the types of additional information and exhibits which will be required from the sponsor. The necessary material is outlined on the application from (2013 Rev) for the various stages of processing. Only the material requested for the particular stage (conditional or firm) is necessary, although any exhibits already available should be furnished.

For Below Market Interest Rate (BMIR) projects and Rent Supplement projects, FHA will determine the availability of mortgage or Rent Supplement funds prior to the Feasibility Conference wherever its analysis indicates a feasible project.

6. Following the Feasibility Conference where agreement has been reached on all of the matters discussed above, a Feasibility Letter will be issued to the sponsor. This letter includes not only the rents, dollar limitations on cost, mortgage and land value and the cash requirements, but also the expected processing time and target date for sponsor submissions. Wherever possible an FHA design representative will be assigned to the project as well.

VI. Development of Forms, Drawings and Exhibits

The decision as to whether the proposal can move to either conditional or firm commitment will be dependent upon the extent of the sponsor's preparation. Assuming that preparation up until now is at the minimum required for determination of feasibility, the sponsor will move to a conditional commitment and then to the firm commitment. (The sponsor with a complete package, it must be emphasized, can move from initial contact to firm commitment directly. The description of the complete step-by-step process is for illustration purposes only. Complete processing flexibility, tailored to the sponsor's preparation and degree of sophistication, is an outstanding feature of AMP.)

The sponsor will submit to the FHA the forms, drawings, and exhibits agreed upon at the Feasibility Conference and listed on the application form (2013) within the time agreed upon. FHA project processing to the conditional commitment will require generally less than 30 days following the case submission by the sponsor. After the processing is completed, FHA will telephone the sponsor to schedule a Conditional Commitment Conference. The Conditional Commitment Letter will be issued and its provisions discussed with the sponsor. This document is non-transferable. During this conference FHA will also provide the sponsor with a Contractor's Cost Analysis, form 2536. The mortgagee will be invited to submit an application with fee with the final contract drawings and documents.

An important shortcut in Accelerated Multifamily Processing is accomplished by the FHA Design Representative discussing proposed plans with the sponsor's architect in the latter's own office, whenever possible.

Although the FHA Design Representative will in no instance approve or sign plans, he will answer any questions about compliance with FHA regulations and consult, where necessary, to assure design of a project on which FHA can insure a mortgage. The FHA Representative will be available for consultation on both preliminary and design development plans.

VII. Final FHA Review and Issuance of a Firm Commitment

When the final contract drawings and documents are complete, certified, and endorsed, the FHA approved mortgagee submits them to FHA for final review and pays his application and commitment fee. FHA will review the documents and issue a firm commitment to the mortgagee.

VIII. Responsibilities and Obligations of Sponsors

The liberal financing under the FHA mortgage insurance program imposes certain responsibilities and obligations on all sponsors. The basic description and outline material indicated below pertain to rental housing under all sections of the National Housing Act. The most important of these responsibilities and obligations are:

1. Equal Opportunity in Housing

FHA regulations require that neither the sponsor nor anyone authorized to act for him will decline to sell, rent, or otherwise make available any of the properties or housing in a multifamily project to a prospective purchaser or tenant because of his race, color, creed, or national origin. The sponsor must further agree to comply with state and local law and ordinances prohibiting discrimination.

2. Prevailing Wage Requirements

On a multi-family project, FHA will not issue insurance of a mortgage loan or an advance thereof unless the principal contractor certifies that all laborers and mechanics will be paid not less than the prevailing wage in the project area and accepts the responsibility for such payment by all subcontractors. Prevailing wages are determined by the Department of Labor and issued to the contractor for his use.

3. Fair Employment Practice

FHA policy requires that ".... There shall be no discrimination against any employee who is employed in carrying out work receiving FHA assistance, or against any applicant for such employment, because of race, creed, color or national origin. ...." The mortgagor must also agree to include this policy in all contracts and subcontracts.

4. Cost Certification Procedure

All FHA insured projects, except sales type cooperatives, are subject to cost certification. After project completion, the sponsor (mortgagor) must certify to the actual cost of the project including fees, charges, and off-site construction cost. For most non-profit mortgagors and all identity of interest builder-sponsors, the contractor and mortgagor must certify to the actual cost of the project.

5. Family Housing

The National Housing Act, as amended (except Sections 213, 231, 232, and Title XI), requires that no mortgage is to be insured unless the mortgagor certifies that he will not discriminate against families with children and will not sell the property while the mortgage is in effect to anyone who will so discriminate.

6. Hotel and Transient Use

With the exception of Section 232 and Title XI, only projects with accommodations suitable for permanent residence are eligible for FHA insurance. The project can not be operated for hotel or transient use.

7. Commercial Facilities

With the exception of projects located in Urban Renewal areas, only commercial facilities adequate to serve the needs of the project's occupants may be included. Commercial areas should not normally exceed ten per cent of the total gross floor area of the project and commercial income should not normally exceed ten per cent of the estimated total gross project income. For projects located within an Urban Renewal area consult the local insuring office for additional guidelines.

8. Rent Ceiling on FHA Projects

With the exception of Sections 213, 231, 232, and Title XI, gross rentals in an FHA project shall not exceed the rentals determined by FHA to be necessary to meet all expenses, reserves, mortgage obligations and a reasonable return. If operating expenses exceed the estimates, or if they increase for reasons beyond the sponsor's control, provisions may be made for increasing the rent ceiling.

9. Annual Financial Statements

Profit and loss statements and balance sheets are required annually on each insured project. In most cases it is required that these be certified by a CPA or licensed Public Accountant.

10. Occupancy Surveys

Annually a form is mailed to all sponsors of FHA-insured projects to determine occupancy ratios and rentals by type of unit.

Architectural, legal and organizational fees are the responsibility of various local offices who know local practices and in general the scale has been found adequate by architects and lawyers who specialize in the field.

Builders who build not for their own account but to re-sell to non-profit sponsors such as churches, unions, co-ops, etc., will not own the job when they are through, so the fact that the job is being built with little or no equity does not interest them.

Builders for non-profit sponsors, on the other hand, are entitled to builder's fees which are based on the dollar amounts of construction costs involved and range from a low of 3% or 4% on the really large jobs, to as high as 10% on the smaller jobs (which might be in the $100,000 or $150,000 area). The legal, organizational and architectural fees vary similarly, depending on size and regional practice.

§ 220

ONE-FAMILY URBAN RENEWAL HOMES [1,2,3]

Purpose of Loan[4]:   To finance proposed, under construction or rehabilitation of one- and two-family

159

housing in approved Urban Renewal areas or acquisition of existing one- and two-family housing constructed or rehabilitated pursuant to approved Urban Renewal plan.

Maximum Amount Insurable:

Occupant mortgagor:
$30,000—one-family;
$32,500—two- or three-family;
$37,500—four-family;
$7,000 per family, over four;

Non-occupant mortgagor:
Property held for rental purposes;
$27,900—one-family;
$30,200—two- or three-family;
$34,800—four-family;
$6,500 per family over four;

Property held for sale to owner-occupant:
$25,500—one-family;
$27,600—two-family.

Loan Value Ratios:

Occupant Mortgagor:
Proposed construction or completed more than one year: 97% of $15,000 of estimated replacement cost plus 90% of cost above $15,000 but not over $20,000 plus 80% of cost above $20,000.

Under construction or completed less than one year: 90% of estimated replacement cost up to $20,000 plus 80% of cost above $20,000.

Rehabilitation:
Construction under FHA or VA inspection or completed more than one year: 97% of $15,000 of estimated rehabilitation cost plus estimated value before rehabilitation plus 90% of such sum above $15,000 but not over $20,000 plus 80% of such sum above $20,000 or estimated rehabilitation cost plus amount required to re-finance debt on property, whichever is less.

160

Not constructed under FHA or VA
inspection or completed less than one year:
90% of $20,000 of estimated rehabilita-
tion cost plus estimated value before
rehabilitation plus 80% of such sum above
$20,000, or estimated rehabilitation cost
plus amount required to re-finance debt on
property, whichever is less.

For veterans:
Loan ratios as provided under § 203(b)
will apply.

Non-occupant mortgagor:
Property held for rental purpose:
93% of amount computed under any above
formulae, but not to exceed estimated
rehabilitation cost plus amount required
to re-finance debt on property.

Property (one- or two-family) held for
sale to owner occupant:
85% of amount under any of above
formulae, but not to exceed estimated
rehabilitation cost plus amount required
to finance debt on property, or amount
available to occupant mortgagor under
any of above formulae, subject to at
least 15% escrow, whichever is less.

Term of Loan: Occupant or non-occupant mortgagor,
except operative builder: 30 years,
except 35 years if mortgagor is unacceptable under 30-year term for housing
built under FHA or VA inspection, or
3/4 of remaining economic life, whichever is less.

Operative builder:
20 years or 3/4 of remaining
economic life, whichever is less.

Interest rate: 6%

Insurance Premium: 1/2% on declining balances.

Initial Service
    Charge:

$20 or 1%, whichever is greater
or
$50 or 2-1/2%, whichever is greater, if mortgagee makes partial disbursements and property inspections during construction.

Fees:

$45—proposed;
$35—existing.

[1] Eligible for open-end advances.

[2] Certification to mortgagor of FHA appraisal amount or estimate of replacement cost is required on one- and two-family housing.

[3] Builder warranty is required on proposed construction one- to four-family housing.

[4] Property must be located in an approved Urban Renewal, redevelopment or code enforcement program area or urban area receiving rehabilitation assistance as a result of natural disaster.

§ 220

MULTI-FAMILY URBAN RENEWAL[1]

Purpose of loan[2]:

To finance construction of rehabilitation of detached, semi-detached, row, walk-up or elevator type rental housing which may include non-dwelling facilities, in Urban Renewal areas—two units or more.

Maximum amount
    insurable[3]:

$30,000,000—private mortgagor;
$50,000,000—public mortgagor;

Elevator type:
$10,500—no bedroom;
$15,000—one bedroom;
$18,000—two bedroom;
$22,500—three bedroom;
$25,500—four bedroom or more.

All other types:
$ 9,000—no bedroom;
$12,500—one bedroom;
$15,000—two bedroom;
$18,500—three bedroom;
$21,000—four bedroom or more.

Loan value ratios:	Proposed construction: 90% of estimated replacement cost.
	Under construction: 90% of estimated value when completed.
	Rehabilitation: 90% of estimated rehabilitation cost plus 90% of estimated value before rehabilitation, subject to following limitations:
	Property to be acquired: 90% of estimated rehabilitation cost plus the lesser of 90% of purchase price or 90% of estimated value before rehabilitation.
	Property owned: estimated rehabilitation cost plus the lesser of debt on property or 90% of estimated value before rehabilitation.
Term of Loan:	Satisfactory to FHA commissioner (usually 40 years or 3/4 of remaining economic life, whichever is less).
Interest rate:	6%
Insurance Premium:	1/2% on declining balances.
Initial Service Charge:	2%
Fees:	Application and commitment: $3 per $1,000
	Separate inspection fee: As set by FHA, but not to exceed $5 per $1,000.

[1] Cost certification is required.

[2] Property must be located in an approved Urban Renewal, urban redevelopment, or code enforcement program area, or urban area receiving rehabilitation assistance as a result of natural disaster.

[3] (a) Family unit limits for two, three, four or more bedrooms may be increased by 25% if the project is to be rehabilitated and has five or less units; (b) family unit limits may be increased up to 45% in high-cost construction areas.

§ 221(d)(3)

BELOW-MARKET RATE MULTI-FAMILY HOUSING FOR LOW-INCOME FAMILIES[1,2,3]

Purpose of loan:

To finance construction or rehabilitation of rental or cooperative detached, semi-detached, row or walk-up housing for low- or moderate-income families or individuals 62 or older or handicapped, with priority in occupancy to those displaced by Urban Renewal or other governmental action.

Up to 10% of the units may be occupied by low- or moderate-income individuals under 62.

Maximum amount Insurable[4]:

$12,500,000
$ 8,000—no bedroom;
$11,250—one bedroom;
$13,500—two bedroom;
$17,000—three bedroom;
$19,250—four bedroom or more.

Loan value ratios:

Public, non-profit, co-operative, builder-seller or investor-sponsor mortgagor:

Proposed construction:
Estimated replacement cost.

Rehabilitation:
Estimated replacement cost plus estimated value before rehabilitation, subject to the following limitations:

(1) Property to be acquired: estimated rehabilitation cost plus the lesser of purchase price or estimated value before rehabilitation.

(2) Property owned: Estimated rehabilitation cost plus the lesser of existing debt on property or estimated value before rehabilitation.

(3) Five times the estimated cost of rehabilitation.

(4) Re-Financing: Debt on property or appraised value, whichever is less.

Limited distribution mortgagor:

Proposed construction:
90% of estimated replacement cost.

Rehabilitation:
90% of estimated rehabilitation cost plus 90% of estimated value before rehabilitation, subject to the following limitations:

(1) Property to be acquired: 90% of estimated rehabilitation cost plus the lesser of 90% of purchase price or 90% of estimated value before rehabilitation.

(2) Property owned: Estimated rehabilitation cost plus the lesser of debt on property or 90% of estimated value before rehabilitation.

(3) Five times the estimated cost of rehabilitation.

(4) Re-Financing: Debt on property or 90% of appraised value, whichever is less.

Builder-seller or investor-sponsor mortgagor subject to 10% escrow.

Term of Loan: Satisfactory to commissioner (usually 40 years or 3/4 of remaining economic life, whichever is less).

Interest rate:	6% which is reduced at final endorsement of mortgage for insurance to 3%.
Insurance premium:	Waived by FHA commissioner.
Initial service charge:	2%
Fees:	(a) Application and commitment: $3 per $1,000.
	(b) Separate inspection fee: as set by FHA but not to exceed $5 per $1,000.

[1]Cost certification required.

[2]Property must be located in community certified by Secretary, Department of Housing and Urban Development, as having a "workable program."

[3]Data on Rent Supplement Program, which follows.

[4]Limits per family unit may be increased up to 45% in high-cost construction areas. Income limits also limit amount of mortgage by limiting rents (check your local office for applicable amounts, your area).

Rent Supplement Program

The Housing and Urban Development Act of 1965 includes authorization for the Secretary, Department of Housing and Urban Development, to make payments to owners of authorized multi-family rental projects to supplement the rentals eligible tenants can afford to pay. The rental projects must be part of an approved workable program for community improvement or approved by local governmental officials. FHA form 2504 contains a detailed discussion of this program.

Eligible Projects

Basic program—§ 221(d)(3) (market interest rate) covers proposed or rehabilitation of multi-family housing project with private non-profit, limited distribution or co-operative housing corporation mortgagor for which the mortgage was insured after August 10, 1965.

Experimental programs—§ 221(d)(3) (below market interest rate) covers proposed or rehabilitation of project with private non-profit, limited-distribution or cooperative housing corporation mortgagor for which a commitment to insure was issued after August 10, 1965.

§ 231 covers proposed or rehabilitation of project with private non-profit mortgagor for which commitment to insure was issued after August 10, 1965.

Eligible Tenants

To be eligible for rent supplement payments a tenant must be an individual or family that has been determined to have assets and income below the established maximums and must be one of the following: an individual or family displaced by governmental action, 62 years of age or older or whose spouse is 62 or older, physically handicapped, occupant of sub-standard housing, or occupant of housing damaged by a natural disaster. (Tenants other than those eligible for rent supplement payments may occupy units in the project.)

Amount of Payment

The amount of the rent supplement payable for an individual or family is the difference between the rental for the dwelling unit and one-fourth of the tenant's income, except that payment may not be more than 70% or less than 10% of the approved unit rental.

Income and Asset Controls

The Department of Housing and Urban Development will impose controls to prevent payment on behalf of tenants whose income or assets exceed permissible limits after occupancy.

The Housing Act of 1968

§ 235—Interest Subsidy to Encourage Low Income Family Home Ownership:

Purpose: To help low income families buy homes or co-ops. Subsidy payments reduce interest costs to home owners to 1%, with the government paying market interest rates to lenders and the home owner limiting his interest payments to 1%, except as set forth elsewhere herein.

Eligibility: Both individual mortgagors and non-profit co-ops or public bodies or agencies.

Income eligibility emphasizes aid to families with not more than 135% of public housing admission limits. The subsidy is limited to the difference between 20% of the home owner's income, after deducting $300 for each minor child, and the monthly mortgage payment.

Maximum mortgage amounts are $15,000 per unit generally, but $17,500 for families of five or more with additional amounts of $2,500 permissible in high cost areas.

New construction, substantial rehab and existing housing are all eligible.

§ 236—Interest Subsidy on Rental Housing for Low Income Families.

Purpose: To subsidize rental and co-op housing for lower income families through the use of an interest subsidy, by payments to lenders to reduce interest costs to low income families to 1%, where other requirements and limits are met.

Eligibility is restricted to non-profit groups, limited dividend corporations or co-ops.

Income levels, maximum mortgage amounts and eligibility structures are the same as under § 235 above. Similarly, the subsidy limitations are the same as in § 235 above, except that the occupants are expected to pay 25% of their income toward their rent instead of 20% in the case of home owners. Mortgage insurance will also be available under § 236, to enable a co-op or private non-profit organization to purchase a project from a limited dividend owner. Thus, limited dividend owners may conceivably use this program to sell their projects to their tenants.

§ 106—Seed Money and Technical Assistance To Non-Profit Housing Sponsors.

§ 106 provides technical assistance with respect to the construction, rehabilitation and operation of low and moderate income housing by non-profit organizations and authorizes HUD to make 80% interest-free loans to non-profit organizations from a newly created revolving fund to cover planning and pre-construction costs connected with federally assisted programs.

§ 107—Housing Partnerships (the "Comsat of Housing")

§ 107 creates a non-profit, governmentally chartered private corporation to carry out a program of encouraging home ownership at all income levels, preferably in partnership with local private or non-profit organizations.

§ 115 and § 3212—Rehab Loans and Grants

§ 115 authorizes grants for low income home owners of up to $3,000 for rehabilitating real property, authorizes grants to low income home owners where property is uninsurable because of physical hazards, and authorizes grants outside of Urban Renewal (concentrated) code enforcement areas, if needed to bring the property into conformity with public standards.

Loans: Authorizes loans for owner-occupied residential property if certified by the local governing body as containing a substantial number of structures in need of rehab.

Purpose of Loans: To remove violations of local minimum housing or building codes. Authorizes loans for general improvement in Urban Renewal areas where necessary to conform to code requirements or carry out Urban Renewal objectives. Limits residential rehabilitation loans to those whose income is generally within § 221(d)(3) below-market interest rate provisions.

Chapter IX

URBAN RENEWAL IS NOT ALL RESIDENTIAL

Most of this book deals with multi-family housing. Urban Renewal is more than multi-family housing. It is garages, downtown parking, theaters, convention halls and hotels, motels, nursing homes, courthouses, county centers, schools, housing for elderly people, department stores, retail stores, industrial plants and warehouses and many, many more.

Business Properties

In the recent listing of "Land Available in Urban Renewal Project Areas for Private Development," almost every single city that had an Urban Renewal project had commercial and industrial land available.

Thus, there are listed 2.3 million square feet of industrial land in Salinas, California; 33,000 square feet in downtown San Francisco for commercial development; there are over one million square feet in East Hartford, etc., all across the country in the thousands of communities with Urban Renewal activities. We suggest you get the most recent listing by writing to Renewal Administration Assistance in Washington, D. C.

170

Bulletins on available land are published regularly and list not only the single-family and multi-family amounts, but the commercial and industrial sites as well.

Ed Fusco's Experiences

In order to explain commercial Urban Renewal, we invited Edmund J. Fusco, the President of Hammerson, Fusco and Amatruda Corp., of New York, to tell something about his own experiences in commercial Urban Renewal.

Mr. Fusco is a second generation builder. Before getting involved in Urban Renewal, he took in as joint venturers a British-American development company. At the present time, they are completing (or have under construction) over one million square feet of retail space and over one-half million square feet of office space in three downtown Urban Renewal areas: New Haven, Lafayette Plaza (Bridgeport, Connecticut) and Main Place (Buffalo, New York).

Pros and Cons of
Commercial Urban Renewal

In discussing his commercial renewal work, Mr. Fusco pointed out that since he was dealing with commercial tenants and not residential space, his jobs had problems all their own. He also discussed the advantages of commercial over and above multi-family jobs.

To begin with, in no case did he get any FHA financing. His financing was all conventional. This saved him all of the FHA paper work, but faced him and his attorneys with quite a batch of additional paper work, to convince his construction and mortgage lenders that they could go along with some of the onerous title conditions imposed by the municipality.

Urban Renewal Is a Partnership

Ed Fusco's main point—which might very well be the theme of this work—Urban Renewal is a partnership between the developer and a municipality. If your partner is a good one you will do well. If your partner is a poor one, no amount of legal paper work will get the job done or make a dollar for you.

Since it is a partnership between you and the municipality, you give up some of your managerial prerogatives. You are not operating alone. You must consult your partner on esthetic matters, timing matters and financial matters—and you must expect that your partner will not keep you at arm's length, but will cooperate and help you if you get into trouble. You should expect your municipal partner to go to bat with you with other government agencies and with the federal government to do what it can to speed up the job.

Downtown Land in Large Quantities

If you are going to build commercial space, and if you are going to get conventional financing, why get involved in Urban Renewal at all?

Mr. Fusco put it bluntly. In no other way, except through the use of the condemnation powers of the municipality working in an Urban Renewal plan, can you assemble large sites consisting of prime downtown land.

If you were to attempt to buy each of the many hundreds of plots and put them together for a downtown office building, parking complex or department store, you would never get the job done (or the cost would be so prohibitive that you could not afford the site).

By condemning all of the area within certain blocks and writing the land down to its fair market value for re-use, the city assembles for you a key site and makes it available in one piece and at one time. There is just no alternative: You either buy downtown land under Urban Renewal, or you avoid downtown land altogether, if you are seeking large plottage.

Choosing Your "Partner"

You must recognize that the partnership between your development company and the municipality forces you to give up some of your freedom as an entrepreneur. You must recognize that the municipality is a political body and you cannot do things which will embarrass this politically sensitive being. You must now ask permission to take steps in connection with the property you have purchased, whereas you would never consider asking such permission from an ordinary seller. You would just go ahead and do it; but once you are in an Urban Renewal job, you must check out the political aspects of what you are doing and try to smooth the way so that no one is politically embarrassed.

In return for the giving up of some of your ability to "wheel and deal" by yourself, you get certain advantages. You can ask the municipality to go to Washington with you. You can ask the municipality to give you special street permits, to clean up zoning problems, and to go to bat with you before the building department. You can ask the municipality to help you with the utilities and to participate in prestige-building ribbon-cutting ceremonies.

This means that since you are going to be tied together with your partner for many, many years on a day-to-day basis, you want to look at the LPA carefully, to gauge their capabilities, integrity, needs and weaknesses.

Staffing Your Organization

Ed Fusco warned new entries into the Urban Renewal field that the vast amount of detail and the size of the jobs involved require a strong, capable organization. Mr. Fusco's minimal staff requirements would be these:

A financial officer—trained in contracts and complex governmental paper work, as well as in the supervision of accounting and bookkeeping personnel.

Construction people—one or more, with the ability to communicate and coordinate between architects, city, contractors, utilities, etc.

Supervisor for tenant work—this job alone takes the work of one or more full time men.

A capable leasing team or brokerage organization—it's too hard to assemble the skilled people to do office building and chain store and department store leasing. Solicitation of these tenants must be left in the hands of a capable organization that knows how to "close" deals.

Urban Renewal lawyers—trained and experienced not only in conventional real estate work and contracts, but also, if possible, in the technical aspects of Urban Renewal. As Ed Fusco pointed out, the redeveloper must have absolute confidence in the ability of his attorneys, because it would be impossible for the developer to read all the documents he must sign, let alone understand them.

Public relations counsel—trained and experienced not only in publicity and presentation work, but also, if possible, experienced in the Urban Renewal field. It is important to prepare the general public for the project, to minimize public opposition, to support the leasing program, and in retail projects, to promote traffic.

Timing

Ed Fusco predicts that large interrelated commercial projects take 2-1/2 to 4 years. Unusual challenges are faced. For example, top skills in architectural work are demanded.

The municipality wants a showpiece. You, on the other hand, need an economical structure. Your architect must be able to balance both of these needs. On the architectural team you will generally need a "name" architect. Many of the problems which arise when a talented and imaginative architect has an eyeball-to-eyeball confrontation with the Local Public Agency disappear if the architect is a member of a prestigious, big-name architectural firm. The LPA is less likely to challenge the recommendations of a big name than those of an unknown.

Parking Problems

All downtown Urban Renewal work, whether office building or commercial, faces the problem of downtown parking. A suggestion from Mr. Fusco to consider is the technique of having the city build the parking (by using its tax-exempt bonds) and leasing it back to you.

The result is a lower cost to you; this parking benefit can then be passed along to the tenants.

Conclusions

Urban Renewal work is difficult but the rewards are there. If you are solidly financed, the returns can be excellent. You can deal with top tenants; the trend is now back to the renewed downtown areas. Mortgage lenders are more readily available, in the renewed downtown area, for commercial tenancy than for the farm lands of exurbia. The proof of the pudding is that Ed Fusco is looking for more Urban Renewal work and would "do it again."

Chapter X

TAX ADVANTAGES AND PITFALLS
IN URBAN RENEWAL

This section will deal with some of the tax considerations facing the Urban Renewal developer. We will not repeat the discussion of depreciation of Urban Renewal, to the extent that material has been covered in earlier sections of this work.

On the other hand, we will take you through some of the decisions on selecting the tax entity (in whose name shall title be; who shall receive the benefits of tax deduction?). We will cover some of the problems involved in the use of corporate entities, dummies, etc.; some of the difficulties involved in allocating depreciation between venturers, and in such items as the tax aspects of builder's fees, collapsible corporations and sub-chapter S.

Maximizing Depreciation

All of you know that depreciation may be computed on a number of different methods: straight line, declining balance method, sum of the digits, and components. Detailed depreciation tables comparing the number of dollars of depreciation available at the end of each of various years and on a cumulative basis may be found in most published income tax services. We will not require them here.

176

The purpose of those tables is to tell you (or your tax consultant) which depreciation technique will give you the most deductions over a specific period.

Some taxpayers who intend to hold for a great length of time, and possibly never sell, will not be interested in maximizing depreciation in the early years; they may wish to have their depreciation held off until the later years, to match the income flow of another property.

Getting Tax Sheltered Income

On the other hand, most taxpayers prefer to have their money tax sheltered as fully as possible, so that they can get their money back as quickly as possible. They prefer to maximize their depreciation in the early years.

Of course, since most properties show losses during the construction period, the very earliest years may need no depreciation shelter. Tax losses which arise out of the payment of interest and taxes during the construction period may either be written off against other income or may be capitalized and carried forward as part of the depreciation base to be used in later years.

The main trick with depreciation is not to select the method that gives you the most depreciation but to select the depreciation to match the income tax needs of you and your group. In other words, what is the point in generating a tax loss if you have no income to offset it?

Component Depreciation

Not as commonly used as the straight line, declining balance and sum of the digits depreciation is component depreciation. Component depreciation offers the opportunity of breaking apart a structure into its component parts (for tax purposes) and selecting the appropriate depreciation rate for each of the component parts.

If your planned structure involves much short-lived equipment, the total number of depreciation dollars on a component-by-component basis should exceed the flat composite rate given to the entire structure.

Thus, if a $1 million building at a 2% composite depreciation rate (assuming a 50-year life) gives rise to a $20,000 per year depreciation deduction, the same building could easily give a $30,000 or $40,000 a year depreciation if the outer walls were given a 60 to 70 year life, but the air conditioning a 10 year life, the heating and ventilating system a 15 year life, the carpeting and drapes a 5 year life, the electrical work an 18 year life, etc.

If a building has much short-lived equipment in it, breaking it up into its component parts might produce a higher depreciation rate than taking a flat composite rate. Since most developers have the trade breakdowns available to them, using the component method of depreciation can produce maximum depreciation with a minimum of guess work.

What Kind of Ownership Vehicle Shall You Use?

Assuming that you could pick any kind of ownership vehicle you select, which is best for you? Of course, in some types of governmentally insured programs, you may only select a limited dividend type of corporation.

First, there are the non-corporate forms of ownership such as individual ownership, tenancies in common, partnerships (both general and limited), joint ventures, trusts and dummy corporations. Then there are the various forms of ownership taxed as corporations such as single corporations, multiple corporations, sub-chapter S corporations, business trusts and real estate investment trusts.

Once again, it is not the province of this section to make a hard and fast recommendation, because the tax vehicle must be tailored to your particular needs. Nevertheless, you should consider the various vehicles set forth above as well as their particular tax attributes and try to match them to your own personal tax goals or to the goals of your group.

If your transaction is going to have taxable income from the very inception, individual ownership or single corporate ownership might avoid duplicate taxation, depending on the tax brackets of the individual owners of the property.

If the investors are all 70% tax bracket people and if a corporation could keep within the 48% bracket, the corporation might be your answer.

Multiple corporations are often considered because each may stay in a 28% tax bracket. The Treasury Department has attacked multiple corporations, but if there are bona fide reasons for setting up multiple corporations, they may withstand that attack. Builders are winning cases in this field. Remember, each corporation which you organize may save you $7,500 per year in federal income.

Using Up Tax Losses

If you _must_ have corporate ownership and if the property is going to show a tax loss the first half dozen years or so, you must decide on how to put the tax loss to work for you.

In some cases it will be by filing consolidated tax returns in which a money-making corporation owns all the stock of the loss corporations and files consolidated returns.

In the limited partnership field, it has been common to have the builder or developer act as the general partner, with the investors acting as limited partners. The tax loss can then be allocated among the general and limited partners, in accordance with the partnership agreement. This will give to the investors as much tax shelter as possible, since they will probably be in the highest tax brackets.

The result, of course, could be reversed with the general partner getting most of the depreciation and the investors getting little, if their needs are different or if the bargaining edge is owned by the general partner.

Tax Importance of Arm's Length Agreements

Whatever the case may be, it is important that the partnership agreement spell out the pattern as to who is to get the depreciation benefits. The Treasury Department will ordinarily recognize the allocation formula set forth in the partnership agreement, unless it is purely set up for tax avoidance purposes. Generally, you can find business reasons behind your agreement, so that this attack by the Treasury Department need not be successful.

Timing

Your tax planning must be done very early in the transaction—in most cases, before you take title to the land or even enter into a contract to buy it.

Once title gets into a particular name you may have a tax if you attempt to get title out of that name and into someone else's name. So, taking title in a dummy corporate name and then acquiring a mortgage commitment and doing the preliminary planning and financing work may lead to tax complications, since the corporation will become "collapsible." If you try to get title out of the corporation and into the name of a group of investing individuals, you may run afoul of the anti-speculation provisions in the contract which prohibit transfer at a profit until the job is completed.

You will also have the "collapsible" corporation tax problems which may give rise to an ordinary income tax, if you try to get the property out of the corporation and into your name by liquidating the corporation.

Just as your accountants will be laying out a step-by-step budget for your development program, just as your architects will be putting together a production schedule for the building venture, so your tax consultants should be planning a step-by-step analysis of what will happen, in regard to taxes, from the moment you sign contracts until the property is sold later on. If you plan for each transaction in advance, you can minimize taxes.

If you do no planning but simply prepare tax returns after each transaction is closed, nothing can happen except that you will pay top tax dollars on anything you do. With rates going to 70% today, no one can afford to put in the years of work in an Urban Renewal job without coming out with the maximum tax benefits on the bottom line. If you spend years trying to plan and consummate the job, spend a little time on getting the best tax consultation you can get so that you, the developer, can keep some of the rewards of your work.

Dummy Corporate Traps

Even a simple transaction like putting title in a corporate dummy's name is fraught with tax complications today. Suppose the dummy takes title and holds title throughout the construction period, taking down the mortgage payments and using them to pay the contractors and insulate the investors from possible liability.

When the project is finished, the corporation transfers title to the individual stockholders so that they can hold the property in their own names and get the depreciation deductions as well as having the income flow to them directly without passing through a double tax at the corporate level.

Does it sound simple? You just set up a dummy corporation and when the job is finished, transfer title to the real owners.

Losing Your Deductions

This kind of routine transaction has been used for many, many years. The only trouble with this transaction is that it creates a whole host of sticky tax problems. For instance, how do the individual investors get deductions for the taxes and construction interest paid during the time the job was being built, if the taxes are paid in the name of the dummy corporation?

Is not the corporation entitled to those deductions and not the individual owners? Surely, it would be disastrous for investors who have planned to get their money back out of these tax deductions to discover they have lost them because somebody took title in a dummy name and did not think the tax problem through.

The Risk of An Ordinary Income Tax

Again, if the dummy holds title until the construction job is finished and then liquidates and transfers title to the individual stockholders—was the dummy a "collapsible corporation"? While the question may sound like a lawyer's riddle to you, the significance of the answer is as follows: If the corporation was collapsible when it liquidated, the stockholders got ordinary income.

What is the amount of that ordinary income? It is the difference between the amount the stockholders paid for their stock (usually nominal) and the fair market value of the property at the date of liquidation!

Note that the tax is going to be an ordinary income tax. It is not going to be a capital gains tax. Note that it is not going to be levied just on the cash you received, but on the fair market value of the property.

That is a question about which experts in the Revenue Service and your experts will have to argue in court. No matter how you slice it, the answer to this question can be income tax liabilities running well into six and seven figures! All because someone did not give thought in advance to the "mere" use of a corporate dummy.

Loss of Depreciation

One last problem—although many more are involved—to illustrate the importance of thinking through the use of something as simple as a corporate dummy: If the corporate dummy holds title to the real estate after the structure is finished, is the corporation the "first user" of the property? If the corporate dummy holds title until a certificate of occupancy is issued and if it then transfers title to its stockholders—who is the first user of the building, the corporation or its stockholders?

Only the first user is entitled to take accelerated depreciation at the 200% declining balance method, or the sum of the digits method. Only the first user can use component depreciation (if the Revenue Service's attitude is right). This means that you may be cutting your depreciation deduction by a full 50% merely through the use of a corporate dummy.

We repeat: Spend some time planning your taxes. Work as hard for yourself as for the LPA and your lenders.

Sub-chapter S Corporations

These corporations are commonly used in building ventures. They are referred to occasionally as "pseudo-corporations" or "corporations which are taxed like partnerships." They may effectively pass through to the investor the interest and tax deductions, during the period of construction, as long as no rental income is collected.

Unfortunately, once the corporations begin to collect rental income, they begin to lose their ability to pass through those losses (or profits) to their stockholders. They cease to be "S" corporations once they begin to collect substantial amounts of rental income.

So, although the S corporation is helpful during the construction period, it becomes a burden thereafter, unless you have planned to control your timing carefully. If you plan for it in advance, you can solve most of these problems, but if you overlook them you will be locked into a trap.

Builder's Fee and Depreciation Problems

Many Urban Renewal developments are built by a "marriage" of a skilled developer or builder to an investor group. If the developer gets a "builder's fee," he will have ordinary income out of it.

Since Urban Renewal fees run into six and seven figures, the builder would be doing an awful lot of work for nothing if he has to give away 70% of it at ordinary income tax rates.

The builder is involved in a constant search for a way to get his fee out as a capital gain or to pay no tax on it at all until he sells off his interest in the property at a later date. Even then he hopes to get a capital gain out of it. The latter course of action involves postponement of any present tax and deferment of the capital gain tax.

Taxes here depend on setting up the transaction properly. If the joint venture contract says that the developer will get X dollars as a fee for doing building work, you can be sure he will wind up with an ordinary income tax. Even the receipt of free corporate stock for services in the venture will be deemed ordinary income. The use of common and preferred stock (or notes) with the senior securities going to the investors will prevent the corporation from getting the benefit of the so-called sub-chapter S election outlined above. A free interest in a partnership, in return for services, is also ordinary income.

In spite of all these problems, solutions have been available for builders and investors to blend their skills and money without tax consequences.

How the transaction would be handled in your particular case would depend on the nature of the joint venture, the interests of the parties and the kind of vehicle you are using.

You will surely review these matters with your attorney and tax consultant because they will be an indispensable part of the joint venture agreement. This kind of agreement must also be thought through at the beginning, since once you enter into one kind of a deal it is difficult to change it into another kind of deal without exposing yourself to tax liability. The sole difference between handling the transaction properly (which can defer all tax until the builder liquidates his entire investment many years hence) and handling it improperly (which may give rise to a huge ordinary income tax in the current year, even though the builder hasn't got a dime to pay it with, since he re-invested it in the deal) is tax planning in advance.

Also, the question of who is to get depreciation on what (the builder versus his investors) and how that depreciation is to be allocated between them should be planned for in advance.

Conclusion

For the third time in this chapter we have stressed that you cannot overlook tax planning and that it must be done early. From your own personal viewpoint, nothing is more important. It can decide whether you wind up broke even after doing a successful job, or wind up a millionaire after doing an unsuccessful one.

Chapter XI

REHABILITATION

Urban planners and local community groups see glamor in rehabilitation. It looks easy; the housing stock is already in existence and, instead of tearing down or running a bulldozer operation, "you just move the families around within the neighborhood while you clean up the apartments and then put the families back in." It consists of up-grading and modernizing rather than destroying and building from scratch.

Unfortunately, it is not that simple. Rehabilitating an old-law, New York City type dumb-bell tenement, which lacked air and light when you began, leaves you with a cleanly painted tenement that lacks light and air when you finish. Painting an apartment that is over-occupied, with too many people per square foot, leaves you a cleaner apartment, at a higher rent, with even more people per square foot, and the cleanliness does not last long in an over-occupied apartment.

Rehabilitating an old building involves problems that cannot be anticipated and costs that cannot be estimated in advance. Old foundations crumble; beams which you counted on as being solid turn out to be rotten, and partitions that you thought you would destroy with a crow-bar turn out to be four feet thick! Joists

185

which you expected to replace turn out to be supported in the adjacent building which does not belong to you, and plumbing which you expected to retain because it looked brand new falls apart when you remove the floor.

Unexpected Costs

Experienced contractors who have run through rehabilitation tell us that the only thing you can expect in rehabilitation is the unexpected. It is true that if you do enough of the same kind of houses over and over again with the same crew, you begin learning how to take short cuts, and you find yourself getting a certain kind of average. If you do thirty or forty of the same style and vintage town house, you will find there are certain problems they all have in common, you will get to know your work, and the fact that one or two of them have aberrations in them will average out insignificantly on a cost basis when spread across many units.

Picking out a single tenement in a morass of slums leaves you with a structure that returns to being part of the slum very quickly. If you don't clean up neighborhoods, little is accomplished in single buildings.

Experienced Contractors

Multi-family rehabilitation requires not only experienced contractors, but cooperation from the municipality. In New York, where charitable foundations cooperated with professional builders and got federal financing and rent supplements, an entire project turned out to be a dismal failure, even though the economics would have led one to expect success, because of lack of coordination between City Departments. Thus, the Rent Administration cut rents and the Building Department delayed re-inspection (which was necessary to boost rents again), so that the foundations were unable to get the funds necessary to continue to carry the structure and went deeply into the hole. Ultimately, they gave up in disgust, because the City's Right-Hand Department did not know what the City's Left-Hand Department was doing.

Careful analysis must be made of the kind of buildings you want to rehabilitate. If you are not planning to do enough rehabilitation work, you will not make enough improvement to warrant

subsidized rentals. If you do too much work, you might just as
well tear the building down and start from scratch. Rehabilitation
of a single building makes little sense, unless something is done
to up-grade at least the whole block—preferably the whole neighborhood.

People Need Rehab, Too

Rehabilitation of structures has failed where there has not
been rehabilitation of people. The formation of block groups
giving the residents civic pride is essential. Social services
must be given at the same time as physical rehabilitation, if the
neighborhood is to be truly improved in any but a superficial
manner. Superficial physical improvement alone deteriorates
very rapidly when no one cares.

Another problem of rehabilitation is that it is a very slow
procedure and requires vast amounts of capital. It has been
stated that if each of the country's top 500 corporations purchased
and restored five old-law Manhattan tenements, it would take over
thirty years before all pre-1900 housing stock in Manhattan was
rehabilitated (and nothing is being said about the Bronx and
Brooklyn tenements). It would take fifty more years to clean up
and up-date the buildings that were constructed from 1900 to 1939.

One of the problems in rehabilitation is the high cost. A
study of rehabilitation across the country—full and complete
rehabilitation—has indicated that the cost of rehabilitation, in many
cases, closely approaches the cost of a new structure. A study of
fourteen FHA mortgage projects in New York City showed average
costs running from $3,000 to $4,000 per room and from $12,000
to $18,000 an apartment. Such costs make one wonder whether
rehab is worthwhile.

Financing Rehab

In brief sketch form only, we have set forth below some of
the financing devices available in rehabilitation. In some cases,
we have given a brief thumbnail sketch; in other cases, we merely
cross-reference you to other sections of this book where there is
a more detailed discussion of the program.

Turnkey Rehab

See the chapter on turnkey (Chapter XIII). Because of flexible architectural standards, turnkey offers a unique opportunity to rehabilitate large numbers of structures. Philadelphia has had the most practical experience in the field, and several thousands of units have already been rehabilitated and turned over to the L. H. A. with full financing coming from HUD.

Conventional Multi-
Family Financing

This is usable only in neighborhoods that are going up, rather than those that are going down. Conventional financing has been competitive with FHA and state programs in areas that have turned around and are starting up-hill. In New York, for example, sections of Chelsea and the upper West Side are now starting to come back, and conventional financing is available. Similar phenomena have occurred in Philadelphia, Washington, D. C., and in Baltimore, where fringe areas downtown have started to come back. Increasing land values are the only hope of conventional financing.

Rehabilitation Grants

HUD has a so-called R. A. A. program offering grants of $1,500 (not to exceed the actual cost of repairs and improvements) to applicants who wish to improve their own homes. These are dealt with under § 115 of the 1965 Housing Act and the more recent amendments, and deal with families having a maximum gross income of $3,000 or less; or, if the income exceeds $3,000 per year, whose monthly housing expense, with the rehabilitation, will exceed 25% of their yearly income. As far as construction standards are concerned, the rehab need only conform to local code requirements and/or with the applicable requirements of an Urban Renewal plan. Information on local programs is usually obtainable from the LPA. The R. A. A. program is limited to Urban Renewal or Code Enforcement areas and to owner occupants of one- or two-family homes.

§ 312
Rehab Loans

This program is available to rehabilitate all kinds of residential properties by direct loan, as distinguished from grants under § 115. The property must be located either within an improved Urban Renewal or Code Enforcement area and must be found to be acceptable as a loan risk.

The different kinds of loans are based on whether the borrower is an owner occupant of one- to four-family property or an investor in such property. Owner-occupied one- to four-family units can receive loans ranging from a maximum of $10,000 on a one-family home to $37,500 on a four-family home, with 45% more available in high cost areas. However, in no case may the loan exceed the cost of the rehabilitation or an overall ceiling of $30,000 for the R.A.A. loan plus the remaining debt, in the case of a one-family structure; $32,500 for a two- or three-family structure; and $37,500 for a four-family structure. There are further limitations, ranging from 80% to 97% of the "as is" value of the property plus the cost of rehabilitation.

Investor-owned properties seeking rehabilitation loans under § 312 are limited to $10,000 per dwelling unit, which can be increased up to 45% in high cost areas to $14,500. Additional loan limitations are that the loan may not exceed the lowest of:

(a) actual rehabilitation cost;

(b) a figure ranging from $30,000 for a single family residence to $37,500 for a four-family residence;

(c) 90% of the estimated cost of rehabilitation plus the estimated "as is" value of the property.

"Per family unit" limitations are also in force. Loan-term limits are a maximum of twenty years or three-fourths of the remaining economic life of the structure. Interest rates under § 312 can be as low as 3%.

§ 502
Rural Housing Loans

§ 502 loans are available to applicants who are unable to

obtain the credit they need from private and cooperative lenders in communities with populations of 5,500 or less. Borrowers must be rural residents who will become the owners of the structures. There are no maximum loan limitations, but since the loans are available only to those people in rural areas who can't otherwise obtain credit, the program is necessarily limited to low-cost structures with a maximum term of thirty-three years. The loan value ratio can be up to 100% of the appraised value after improvements. Over $350 million of loans were issued in a recent year under § 502. Further information is available from the local Farmer's Home Administration Office or by writing to the Farmer's Home Administration, Department of Agriculture, Washington, D. C.

FHA Programs

§ 203(b) financing is available in connection with one- to four-family housing, and, although we are basically dealing with the acquisition of a proposed or "under construction" house, the program may also be used to re-finance existing housing or to pay for repairs, alterations or improvements. Thirty- or thirty-five year loans are available with a maximum at three-fourths of the remaining economic life up to the first 97% of the appraised value.

§ 203(k) Loans

§ 203(k) loans are to finance alteration, improvement or existing housing at least ten years old where the mortgagor is either an owner or a tenant of the housing in question; and, if a tenant, with a lease extending at least ten years beyond the maturity of the loan. Loan limitations range from $10,000 for a one-family house to $37,500 on a four-family house which may be increased 45% in high construction cost areas. The maximum term of the loan is twenty years or three-fourths of the remaining economic life.

Since discounts and pre-payment penalties are prohibited under § 203(k), the program has had little use to the present time.

§ 220

§ 220 covers one- to eleven-family housing, with loan limits similar to the previous sections. It is limited, however, to Urban

Renewal and Code Enforcement areas, and the program has not had much utilization because it competes with outright grants and low income (§ 221(d)(3)) loans available under various other federal programs.

§ 220 is available for all residential construction, to finance rehabilitation in Urban Renewal areas. These loans are available to investors, builders, developers or individual owners in amounts ranging from $9,000 to $21,000 in no-bedroom to four-bedroom units, and from $10,000 to $25,500 in elevator-type units, with increases of up to 45% in high cost construction areas. Loan value ratios go to 90% of estimated rehabilitation cost, plus 90% of estimated value before rehabilitation.

This program has languished or flourished, depending upon the relationship of the statutory interest rate permitted to the money market. If the rate is considered good on a government guaranteed obligation at the time, the program is utilized; but if the interest rate is not competitive, the program languishes. In short, construction advances are available and coordination with the LPA is required, since the program is limited to Urban Renewal areas.

§ 220(h)

§ 220(h) essentially provides second mortgage or supplemental money and does not require re-financing of outstanding indebtedness; loans are for up to twenty years, with maximum loan amounts of $10,000 per unit. 10% builders' and sponsors' profit and risk allowances are permitted; and these loans are available to investors, builders, developers or individual owners. Eligibility is restricted to Urban Renewal areas or Code Enforcement areas.

Chapter XII

LEASING IN URBAN RENEWAL

Urban Renewal land may be leased as well as purchased.
Provisions for leasing Urban Renewal land have been found in all
the laws since the Housing Act of 1949. A number of LPA's have
negotiated long-term leases in preference to sales. We are going
to look at leasing, from the developer's viewpoint, although we
will attempt in this section to point out some of the pros and cons
of leasing from LPA's viewpoint.

The Romance of Leasing

From the redeveloper's viewpoint, a long-term lease of 40
years or more with options to renew past that point, and possibly
with options to purchase the land at a fixed price can offer an
advantageous financing plan.

Let's begin by looking at it this way: If the redeveloper buys
the land, he will have to come up with the full purchase price for
it. He may fund that purchase price by mortgaging; but unless he
gets a 100% mortgage, he is going to have some of his capital tied
up in the land, in any event. By leasing the land, his total charges
over the long term may be higher, but his current equity is freed
for use elsewhere.

192

Leasing Can Be Cheaper
Than Buying

If the redeveloper is able to get a 100% mortgage, leasing may still be better than buying, because leasing may offer the opportunity of deducting the entire rent bill on your tax return, while buying gives you non-depreciable land with only the interest portion of your mortgage payments deductible; the mortgage amortization payments will not be deductible.

Even the annual leasing charges can be less than the annual mortgage charges—aside from the saving in equity. Urban Renewal leasing is handled in the following manner:

How Leasing Can Save You Money

Assuming you wish to lease a piece of Urban Renewal land from an LPA, the first question that comes up is—how will the LPA finance the current acquisition cost of the land, if all the LPA is going to get are the annual rental payments from you as a long term tenant?

The technique that has been evolved for financing land leases is for the LPA to issue bonds, which are guaranteed by the federal government, to finance the acquisition cost of the land. Thus, the government can repay the advances it has made, in the same manner as if the land had been sold. This is an over-simplification of a complicated procedure, but the last few sentences outline the basic methods of handling leasehold financing.

There is an acquisition; a leasing; and, finally, a sale of bonds which are paid for out of the rent payments and guaranteed by the government.

An Example of Leasing at Work

Assume that the LPA has in its inventory a $1 million piece of land, and that a redeveloper approaches it with the suggestion that a 50-year lease be made on the land at an annual rental of 5% of the $1 million value, or $50,000 per year. The redeveloper also wants the option to purchase the land at any time during the 50 years at $1 million.

The first problem that arises is: How will LPA get the $1 million to reimburse it and the federal government for their respective shares of the $1 million land cost (which would ordinarily have been raised by selling the land if the developer hadn't asked to lease).

The answer is for the LPA to prepare a bond issue of $1 million, using the $50,000 rentals to pay both interest and amortization on that bond issue year after year over the 50-year life of the lease.

How It's Done

Such an amount (5% per annum) would be enough to amortize interest and principal on the 50-year bond issue, assuming a 4% interest rate. Actually, the figures I have given you here have been rounded out.

The point I am trying to make is this: It is feasible for a 4% interest rate to be used on those bonds since they are tax exempt municipals, and their yield to a 50% tax bracket investor would be the equivalent of 8%. The bonds are guaranteed by the United States, through HUD (issued by the LPA).

Thus, because of the municipality's borrowing power at low interest rates, the 5% annual rental would represent a substantial saving in annual payments to the redeveloper tenant.

Even if the developer had put up no cash to buy the land, and even if he could get a 100% mortgage on it for 40 years, it is doubtful that he could get an interest rate of lower than 6% with probably 1-1/4% amortization requiring constant payments of 7-1/4%. This would call for $72,500 of annual payments instead of $50,000 of annual payments. Thus, the lease helps the cash flow by cutting the annual payments through the use of the municipality's lower interest rate, plus the tax advantage to the developer which comes from the entire $50,000 of annual payments being deductible (whereas the 1-1/4% mortgage amortization in the purchase deal would not be deductible).

194

Leasing Versus Buying

The test, then, from the redeveloper's viewpoint, is: Can leasing generate a better cash flow than purchasing? There are other tests, also. For example, a long-term leasehold is a complicated document. There is no point in kidding ourselves, it is going to take much longer to clear the paper work through the LPA, HUD, the FHA or a conventional lender than a straight mortgage transaction would.

Leasing's Effect on the Mortgage Loan

The lender will probably make a smaller loan on bricks standing on a leasehold than on bricks standing on fee ownership. What you must do, in each case, is to make your own set of computations and to ask yourself whether a lease is better than a purchase, taking into consideration all the pluses and minuses discussed above.

Of course, a lease that gives you an option to buy seems to to have no minuses. Once again, the Lease may affect the amount of the loan you will get on the rest of the project. Lenders who make loans on leases which involve options to purchase often wonder whether the purchase price should be subtracted from the total loan value.

Three Kinds of Urban Renewal Leases

Three possibilities are available in the field:

(1) A straight lease—That is, a lease for 50 or 99 years with or without options for additional leasehold terms at varying rental rates. Title to the land will revert to the owner at the expiration of the lease. This is a straight leasing transaction. There are no options to purchase.

(2) The lease with an option to purchase—The option may be exercisable anywhere along the length of the term, or at the expiration thereof. Such a lease usually sets forth the price at which the option is to be exercised.

195

(3) The "lease-purchase" transaction—In the lease-purchase transaction, when the lease expires you get the fee without further payment. In other words, if you make all the rental payments called for under the lease, the fee comes to you as a "gift" at the expiration of all the payments. This last kind of transaction is really nothing but an installment sale. You should know that if you are going to do FHA financing your lease will have to have in it an option permitting the FHA to purchase, in the event of a default by the leasehold tenant.

The Lease as a Disguised Option

The lease with the option to purchase is an interesting document. HUD's Urban Renewal regulations prohibit the granting of options on Urban Renewal land. This is to prevent speculation and the tying up of property while nothing is happening on it. A lease with an option to purchase is really nothing but an option.

While the tenant who walks away from his lease will be dropping his rental money, you could consider such payments as payments for the option. If the rental does not start right away, you might really have a free option. At least, you should so consider the transaction.

Whether you will be able to work this out in a specific situation or not depends on how difficult a time the LPA is having at marketing the land.

Minimum Sized Leasing Transactions

Another factor you should take into consideration in the leasing field is the size of your transaction. The preparation of a municipal or governmental bond issue is going to take a lot of time and a lot of legal paper work.

On a realistic basis, it is you who will be paying for both of them. You will pay the cost of the legal work (by having your interest rate adjusted to absorb it). You will be paying the cost of the delays by not knowing where you are going until all of the legal problems and red tape are cleared away.

So, we suggest not using the lease and bond issue on any transaction involving less than $1 million worth of land. Indeed, the transaction should probably involve more money than that.

As an economic matter, it would hardly seem to make sense on a smaller transaction.

Some Particular Leasehold Drafting Problems

As soon as you divide the values and responsibilities relating to a piece of land between you, the redeveloper as a tenant, and the LPA as a landlord, a large number of practical problems arise. The solutions to those problems will depend on your set of circumstances, but we felt it was most important to raise the questions for your consideration, if you plan doing a leasehold transaction.

Here are just a few of the questions that you must answer and which you should think about, before entering a leasehold transaction. This is not intended to be a complete checklist. (A 99-year lease on which millions of dollars of construction are going to be placed will run several hundred pages. It will be among the most complicated documents ever drafted by your lawyer.) But, here are a few problems you should think about:

1. What effect is the lease going to have on your rights to mortgage your property? Can you get any kind of leasehold mortgage you want, in any amount? What about subsequent refinancings? Will they be senior to or rank behind the leasehold obligations?

2. What are the fee owner's rights? Can the LPA mortgage the land? If so, will their mortgage be ahead of your mortgage? If the LPA is first in line to mortgage, you are not likely to get much of a mortgage loan yourself, unless you limit their rights.

3. What will happen in case of condemnation? How will the proceeds of a condemnation award be split between you (the redeveloper owning the bricks) and the LPA which continues to own the land?

4. How about casualty insurance proceeds? If there is a fire and a total destruction of the premises, how will the proceeds be divided between you and the LPA fee owner? If you are to get the entire proceeds of the insurance and if you keep those proceeds, how will the fee owner collect his rents with your building gone?

5. What legal restrictions are there on your getting a leasehold loan? In other words, if you do not own the fee, what effect will the banking and insurance of your lender have on the lender's ability to give you the mortgage loan you want?

6. What rights will you, as the leasehold tenant, have to assign your lease, to sell it, or to sublet thereunder? Are you going to have to get anybody's consent? What rights will the fee owner have to object to any subletting you may do? Remember, you may have to make hundreds of subleases. Are you going to need the LPA's consent on each of them?

7. Assuming there are options to renew, how will they be handled? Who will be permitted to exercise such an option (just you, the original tenant, or may a subtenant or an assignee)? To whom should notice of the exercise of the option be sent? To the LPA? What if the LPA is not in existence at the time you exercise the option?

8. What shall the rent be, for successive renewal terms? Shall it be the same rent as the initial term? Shall it be increased to reflect the cost of living? Shall renewal terms involve a lesser rental (since the original rent presumably paid off the bond issue)? What effect can renewal options be given by lenders?

9. Defaults: If the redeveloper defaults, what rights will his mortgage lender have to make good his default, thus keeping the lease in full force and effect? Surely, the mortgage lender needs some protection. What kind of defaults can he cure? What kind will the lender not be permitted to cure? Assuming the lender has the right to cure all of the defaults under the lease, does the lender understand and want to undertake the obligation called for?

10. Subleasing rights: Will the fee owner be able to approve subleases by the redeveloper? Will the redeveloper be able to cancel and modify the subletting by himself? Bear in mind that the sublettings, if properly handled, represent additional security

to the fee owner, helping him make certain that he collects his rent. Mishandled sublettings or mishandled lease modifications may destroy much of the security that assures the fee owner he will collect his rent.

11. Net leases: The lease must spell out carefully each and every obligation of the redeveloper-tenant to make certain that the fee owner (the LPA) involves itself in no obligations and that the obligation to pay rent to the fee owner is unconditional. Each and every charge against the premises must be collectible from the redeveloper-tenant.

12. Technical tax problems: If the fee is owned by the LPA, will it be exempt from real estate taxation (because the real estate is owned by a municipal body) even though it is leased to a redeveloper? This problem should be considered and if, under local law, the property is not subject to real estate taxation, the rental should be increased so that the municipality gets an equivalent income in the form of rent, instead of in the form of taxes.

13. Redeveloper's rights to rebuild or replace planned structures with other structures: In a 99-year lease, two or three successive buildings may rise on the leased fee. What kind of structures shall succeeding buildings be? What shall the redeveloper's rights and obligations be? Who shall approve subsequent structures? What effect will the particular Urban Renewal Plan have on subsequent buildings?

14. Non-rental obligations of tenant: Obviously, if the tenant were being sold a fee pursuant to Urban Renewal plans, his fee would contain a number of limitations and restrictive covenants setting forth exactly what the tenant had to build; when it had to be built by; and containing a number of anti-speculation provisions and other fair labor and employment practice standards.

These same special Urban Renewal and other restrictive clauses must be written into the lease form, so as to restrict the redeveloper-tenant to the Urban Renewal Plan, including all of the statutory conditions and administrative conditions. Will these conditions be acceptable to a leasehold mortgage lender?

Conclusions

Leasing instead of buying Urban Renewal land should be considered, particularly on larger parcels. Costs can be compared, as well as tax benefits. The drafting problem, though formidable, has been solved by others. You can do the same—if the figures are rewarding enough.

Chapter XIII

THE NEW TURNKEY PUBLIC HOUSING PROGRAM

The Turnkey Program is aimed at supplying housing to the lowest income groups. Welfare and relief clients, the ill, the indigent, and the retired whose low incomes would qualify them for public housing, are the prospective tenants here. The program is called "turnkey" because the builder will deliver the finished product to a local housing authority which will buy it in a completed form so that it need do nothing else but "turn the key" to move in or to move its tenants in.

What's New?

It is a departure from the older local public housing authority practice where the local housing authority (referred to in government jargon and in the rest of this chapter as the LHA) locates a site and either buys it or condemns it, prepares plans and specifications and has a contractor bid in the job and construct it for the LHA which retains title to the land during the construction period. Actually, the new Turnkey Program involves no new statutory authority (the authority has existed since the U. S. Housing Act of 1937), but the program does involve a new emphasis and a new set of administrative techniques that give the Turnkey Program much architectural and land site flexibility, as well as certain unique opportunities to involve private builders or developers.

The Builder-Developer's Role

Basically, the Turnkey Program which will be discussed in this chapter is a program involving the selection of the land site by a builder or developer, offering it to an LHA, preparing a set of plans and specifications for submission to the LHA, and the giving out of the contract work either to third party contractors or the building of the work by the developer with ultimate delivery of the "turnkey" to the LHA. A basic program ordinarily involves the sale of a multi-family development to an LHA. It is an ordinary-income, one-shot proposition for the developer under most circumstances. He does not own the project afterwards: He sells it to the LHA. Developers find in the program an opportunity to keep their organizations going during slack periods and to make sales profits which boost their volume, absorb a portion of their overhead or beef up their organizations.

Included in the Turnkey Program, however, is a leasing program in which the builder may continue to own the project, leasing all or part of it to the LHA and keeping the depreciation and ownership rights for himself. The leasing program involves standard builder investment concepts and will be discussed separately herein.

We will take you through the Turnkey Program step by step, so that you will see how it works, how it is financed, what some of the problems are, and how you can choose the program which most meets your needs. Turnkey is flexible enough to offer opportunities in the rehabilitation of existing structures and gives the LHA and the community sufficient architectural flexibility to avoid the "institutional" look that public housing has had in the past.

Turnkey, Step by Step

The first step, obviously, is to locate a site. Possibly, if you are interested in rehab, you will already own the site and the buildings on it. If you don't own the site, you should have it under option so that the price and terms are fixed before you go to the LHA.

In some cases sophisticated developers will go to the LHA before optioning a site to find out where they would like the housing built and how many units they are looking for. With that information in hand, the builder can go out and option a site.

Go To The LHA

On the other hand, if you already have a site or are contemplating rehab, your first step is to go to the LHA and discuss with them generally how many units they want built; whether they deem the location desirable; what cost limitations might be; whether the LHA has any architectural standards of its own; or whether the LHA wants any unique facilities developed on the premises. After preliminary discussions, if the proposal starts to jell, the builder and the LHA enter into a "letter of intent," in which the LHA agrees to purchase the completed project at a specific price, provided the developer finishes the job in accordance with the plans and specifications annexed. Of course, by that time, the LHA has had its architect work up those plans and specifications (which have moved along from some preliminary layouts and drawings to pretty detailed sets) and has planned and arranged for stand-by construction financing and offered the completed project to the LHA at a specific price on which the builder anticipates he will make a profit.

No Cost Certification

It is most important to note two things in this connection:

(1) The Turnkey Program does not involve cost certification in the same way the FHA programs do. In other words, if the builder is efficient enough to beat standard cost estimates or estimated land values through smart buying or good production, he may keep the excess profit for himself under the Turnkey Program. Under FHA programs, the mortgage would be reduced and he would be somewhat penalized by having this excess value locked into the project as his equity. In turnkey, the builder can profit (and pocket the profit) through his efficiency.

(2) A letter of intent with plans and specifications annexed is
backed by the bonding authority of the LHA and a
commitment against the United States Treasury. That
document, in view of both Treasury Department and LHA
liability, should help the developer obtain construction
loan financing from ordinary commercial mortgage
lenders.

Bankable and Borrowable

While some lending institutions question whether the letter
of intent is a "bankable" document, no one argues that the contract
of sale—the next document discussed herein—is a "bankable"
document. Perhaps the greatest strength of the letter of intent is
that it offers the builder the guarantee that if he spends more time
and money on architectural plans or land buying and if the LHA
walks away from the deal before the contract is signed, the builder
probably has the right to enforce the letter of intent against the
LHA, compelling them to pick up his tab and take over the land
site at its then developmental stage. I say the builder "probably
has the right" because until a builder has been in that position and
tested the matter in the courts, it is difficult to tell. However,
there is no question that once he has a contract, he has an enforceable, borrowable document. Whether the letter of intent is an
enforceable document is a question which can be argued on both
sides of the fence, depending upon whom you talk to and on how
conservative your lawyer is.

Flexibility Under Turnkey

Because the builder is permitted to hire his own architect and
do his own planning, specifying his own materials and utilizing
modern cost cutting techniques including large scale rehabilitation,
it is planned that turnkey will permit:

(a) substantial cost savings estimated at up to 15%;

(b) substantial time savings (as much as two or three years)
by cutting paper work and LHA procedures to the bone;

(c) flexibility in design type, construction techniques and
types of developers taking part in the program (the
program is aimed at encouraging banks, mortgage lenders
and community renewal groups to become involved as
developers).

204

(d) Neighborhood diversification (by permitting developers or LHA's in middle income areas which have been by-passed) which blends lower income families into middle income areas. Thus, high concentrations of poor families in institutional type structures and institutionalized neighborhoods can be avoided.

It is too early to tell yet whether all of these objectives can be met by the program, but these are the turnkey's objectives.

Initial Contact With the LHA

There are over 3,000 LHA's involving almost every city in the country with a population of over 50,000, and quite a number of Indian tribes scattered all across the country. To determine whether a particular LHA plans to get involved in turnkey housing, you should drop in to see your LHA office or visit your HUD Regional Office where you can pick up a list of public housing authorities making applications and reservations (Report S-10, published monthly). Indeed, if your community has no LHA, and if there is a need, HUD has a program and a sample statute to facilitate the organization of such an LHA.

General Requirements of Turnkey

At the first LHA conference, the LHA usually informs the developer of some of the requirements of the program, such as the payment of prevailing wages, room cost limitations, equal opportunity requirements, etc. The LHA will also inform the developer about its general guidelines as to room sizes, special facilities required by the elderly or the handicapped, as well as the LHA's general policies and design requirements. The developer submits a formal proposal which consists of a site plan, the number and size of the proposed dwellings and the related facilities, and outlines specifications or refers to comparable construction projects the builder handled elsewhere, together with the proposed completed "turnkey" sales price. If the LHA is interested, it submits this preliminary material in the form of a development program to the HUD office for approval. The program may include not only housing units, but space for community activities and, under certain specified circumstances, even shops and stores needed by the tenants.   The material submitted to HUD will also be accompanied by evidence that the locality has approved the particular site, if such approval is required by local law.   HUD wants to know that the community is committed to the program before it does its own processing.

HUD Signs Contract Also

If HUD approves the development program, it enters into a financial assistance contract with the LHA covering the LHA's full purchase price of the finished job.   The LHA is now ready to enter into a letter of intent with the developer.   The letter's purpose is to set forth the proposed purchase price, procedures for its adjustment under certain circumstances, a schedule of completion with respect to working drawings and specifications (if they have not already been completed).   The plan is that the letter of intent will be a "bankable" and "bondable" document, and to make the document "bankable" and "bondable, " the plans and specifications are required to be in pretty finalized form.

Of course, the plans and specifications must meet all state and local law requirements, codes and regulations, and they must detail the work to be done and must be prepared under the supervision of a registered architect.

Firming Up The Price

Presumably, the developer is now ready to firm up his price against his final plans and specifications.   The purchase price that the LHA may commit itself to is either the one specified in the letter of intent or the mid-point of two cost appraisals, whichever is lower.   The two appraisals are ordered by the LHA from independent appraisers.   If the mid-point is less than 95% of the price as specified in the original letter of intent and if a price satisfactory to the parties and HUD cannot be negotiated, the developer and the LHA are not obligated to proceed any further.   If the project does not proceed any further, the developer, at his option, may sell the site and the plans to the LHA at the price previously agreed upon for the plans and at either the developer's cost of the land or at the mid-point of the two land appraisals, whichever is lower.   Presumably, this option on the part of the developer to "put" his architectural plans and his land to the LHA are a guarantee to the developer that he will not get stuck for the cost of the architectural work and land acquisition. While not absolutely riskless, the option does protect the developer against the risk that "the slide rule boys" (as they are affectionately called by most builders) will come in with some unrealistically low cost estimates.

Sales Contract

With final plans, cost estimates, etc. available, it is now possible to enter into a sales contract between the LHA and the developer. This document is really a "bankable" document, in our opinion. It is a contract between the LHA and the developer, guaranteed by the credit of the United States Treasury, to the effect that if the developer produces the building called for in the annexed plans and specifications, the LHA will buy it at the price set forth therein, and if the LHA doesn't, HUD will. Having gone this far, construction financing should not be too difficult to get. The contract calls for a more or less conventional one-year clause compelling the developer to remedy defects of materials and workmanship backed up by an escrow or surety bond or by an irrevocable letter of credit or deposit of negotiable securities.

Inspections During Construction

Inspections during construction are made by an independent architect hired by the LHA, and although employees of HUD and the LHA may also make inspections, these are more or less for determining whether agreed-on standards and specifications are being met, and not to substitute the government's judgment for that of the independent architect.

Contract Problems

Completion dates are set forth on a contract, but automatic extensions of the time are provided for when due to delays beyond the developer's control, as well as for delays authorized by the LHA. The contract does specify that HUD will approve change orders only if they involve substantial increases or decreases in the purchase price. The contract further provides for full settlement within the shortest possible time after completion, and completion is based on the obtaining of the usual form of certificate of occupancy, as well as a certification by the LHA's inspecting architect that the property is in good and tenantable condition. Any uncompleted work is listed by the LHA's architect in a "punch list" and the LHA may withhold the estimated amount of cost of completion from the purchase price for minor items.

HUD Legal Opinions

Where a local construction lender is a little hesitant about mortgage financing and is not certain that he has the full faith and credit of the federal government behind the job, HUD is prepared to issue a written legal opinion committing the government thereto. The program contemplates mixed income developments, especially in a leasing program where some apartments will be leased to low income tenants and others not qualifying for low income limitations will be rented to middle income tenants. Thus, the LHA and HUD can provide leasing or funds to fill out the project while the developer may own other units therein.

The Leasing Program

Generally, the developer goes to the LHA and offers to sign a lease on existing buildings, or rehabilitated buildings or on proposed new construction, with the LHA. The lease can be for a block of apartments which will sublease to eligible tenants. Other possibilities include a direct leasing by the owners to low income families with the rent being more or less guaranteed by the LHA.

§ 23 of the Act

Under § 23 of the Housing Act of 1937, as amended in 1965, leases may be for periods of from one to five years and may be renewable up to a maximum of ten years. The leases may include (or may not include) options to the LHA ultimately to buy the property. Other plans involve giving an opportunity to the tenants ultimately to buy their own apartments. The leasing program offers a number of advantages to the community:

    (a) It provides virtually instant housing for families or elderly persons in acute need or about to be displaced by an Urban Renewal project or a natural disaster,

208

because it can draw on existing or rehabilitated housing stock.

(b) Although the rents are subsidized, the properties (which remain in private ownership) continue to pay local real estate taxes.

(c) The rental guarantees by the LHA, backed up by the credit of the United States Treasury under leases of up to five years, offer to the owner a good opportunity to finance any rehabilitation work that may need to be done.

(d) While operating under a government guaranteed rental income program, the owner may find the depreciation or other income tax benefits even more important than the return on his investment.

(e) Theoretically, the program offers an opportunity for tenants who build up their incomes to "graduate" from public to private housing without moving. Under the leasing program, it is possible for tenants whose incomes rise above public housing limits to enter into direct unsubsidized leasing arrangements with the owners of the property, either for rental or to buy their own individual unit under a co-op or condominium plan; or, if the houses stand on their own lots, as an individual home.

Some Practical Experiences
in the Field

Among the LHA's who have had practical experience in the field of turnkey, one finds the Metropolitan Dade County Housing and Urban Development Authority which has engaged in a leasing program of 420 units and is looking for 500 more. When asked why the leasing program was deemed successful, the director pointed out that the developer was guaranteed against any rental loss, since the housing division guaranteed full occupancy for the term of its lease, either supplying subtenants or supplying rent in the event no subtenants were available.

Apartments for Elderly

In the Washington D. C. area, Claridge Towers was one of the country's first experiments. Claridge Towers was not originally intended for public housing, but the 343 units for the elderly was one of the first jobs to clear through the paper pipeline. The site was already owned by the builder and he had submitted detailed plans and specifications to the FHA, planning a 207 type of "luxury" job; but the FHA decided there was an over-supply of luxury efficiency and one-bedroom apartments (contemplated in the plans) in the immediate area and stated it would not like to issue an insurance commitment. Accordingly, when HUD began to move along its Turnkey Program, the builder was able, with only minor modifications, to remove some of the luxury facets such as a swimming pool, etc. and convert his one-bedroom efficiencies to "housing for the elderly" by widening doorways and converting ground floor shops and offices to a social center. In Roseville, Michigan, another housing for the elderly with as few as 44 units got off the ground very early.

Detached Homes

Bossier City, near Shreveport, Louisana, had 25 three-bedroom detached houses delivered to it as a "Turnkey." Located in the suburban subdivision, the homes are indistinguishable as public housing and gave the builder an opportunity to deliver 25 units to the LHA.

In Miami, Florida, not only did the LHA use the leasing program outlined above, but it involved itself in several housing-for-the-elderly projects on a conventional purchase basis. Two-story town houses have gotten the okay in Indianapolis and involved a number of pre-assembled components produced by National Homes Corporation as a demonstration of some of the flexible aspects of turnkey.

Leasing All Around Town

Lorain, Ohio, was one of the first LHA's to push ahead in turnkey leasing and claims that it is responsible for leasing units in all areas of the city including several exclusive residential areas containing homes in the $50,000 class. Typical of the units being leased in Lorain are two-bedroom duplexes and attached houses; and the LHA has taken options to purchase at between $12,500 and $14,000 on duplex units, and as much as $16,500 on $160 rental jobs which involve five-bedroom, split-level houses with 1-1/2 bathrooms on 60 x 125 lots.

Chapter XIV

PUBLIC RELATIONS AND
COMMUNITY PARTICIPATION

With twenty years of Urban Renewal behind us (it's hard to believe it is that long since the Housing Act of 1947 started it all), we have learned a lot, and times have changed. From Urban Renewal programs which were essentially the program of one or more men in a city (such as Robert Moses in New York or Mayor Lee in New Haven), we have moved toward more and more community participation, particularly since the New York and Detroit riots demonstrated that the poor resented having their communities planned for them from the top, without consulting them. As we move away from "benevolent despotism" to "local self-government," a number of difficulties arise:

Power Struggles

Who is the community? In dealing with the poor who, in many cases, have in the past been poorly organized, who represents them? Since many of these communities are just beginning to get themselves organized into power groups, outsiders, such as developers or municipal authorities who enter the area seeking to check out the wishes of the community, have difficulty in deciding who speaks for the community. Does the local church? Does the local congressman or assemblyman? Do the newly organized block groups? Do the little people who turn out in the meetings represent the community? Or does the man from the back of the room who stands up and yells the loudest at the meeting represent it?

Sometimes, in the case of long established ghetto communities, leadership battles have taken place, and the "power brokers" can be located. Yet, in times like these, it is hard to tell whether a long established minority congressman represents his constituents and can speak for them as to whether high-rise or low-rise housing is wanted and whether a school is more important than housing, or vice versa.

The Role of the Minority Employee and Contractor

One of the problems faced in Urban Renewal areas has been the desire to get the residents to lift themselves up by their bootstraps. With the vast expenditures in Urban Renewal, it is anticipated that the flow of those funds will encourage local unemployables or marginal employees to "train up" their skills—first as unskilled building trades employees, then more skilled, then foremen, subcontractors, and finally contractors—in the same way that immigrant groups before them worked their way up the ladder.

Obstacles to Theory

The trouble with the theory has been in the practice. 1970 is not 1890, nor even 1910, and the minority employee who seeks to work his way up that ladder finds all kinds of obstacles.

In many cases, before you can become an unskilled laborer on a construction job, you need a union card. Before you can get a union card, you must take an apprentice test. Before you can take an apprentice test, you must be able to answer questions geared to screen out people of a non-middle-class background or high school education. If you cannot pass the apprentice test, you cannot work on a union job, and if you cannot work on a union job, you cannot work your way up in the construction trades ladder. These are some of the battles faced by minority groups today.

Aside from the pressures on unions to discourage these practices, there has been a pressure on major contractors and on municipalities to give out the construction work to minority contractors or subcontractors. Here, again, one faces problems. To become a major G. C. on an Urban Renewal job, you have to be bondable. If you are not bondable, you cannot get the job. To be bondable, you have to have money. To have money, you have to have had a record of a number of successful jobs on which you made money. You build your way up slowly in the contracting business. Most large contracting organizations started with people who had a formal education or who worked their way up from brick layer to foreman and from foreman to subcontractor and from subcontractor to general contractor over a period of a generation or two.

Union Pressures

Where does a minority group man start today, if he cannot even get a union card? Minority communities have insisted that the subcontract work be given out to minority subcontractors, and, in the last half-dozen years or so, more and more knowledgable people have gone into the minority subcontracting field. "Local participation" is the cry in many urban communities, especially by local community action groups.

The problem from the developer's viewpoint is a simple one: If you are going to build in a minority community, is the minority community going to want participation by local subs? If so, are the local subs as efficient as the people you have been dealing with? Are they bondable? Are they financially stable? If any of these factors are missing or controversial, your costs, as a developer, will be affected. If your costs are affected—if the minority contractor's inexperience turns out to be more expensive than his majority competitor—who is to pay for it? If he has never had any experience before, how will his job work out and who will take the risk of non-performance? Hard and gritty questions like this are looked upon with a jaundiced eye by anything but non-profit groups. Even non-profit groups must perform within a budget.

Non-Profit Sponsorship

In an effort to escape the charge of economic imperialism, many municipalities prefer to deal with non-profit sponsors. Here, again, difficult problems arise. There is no question that a broad-base local church group has a better chance of getting community action and community ratification than a complete outsider. Legislation and administrative regulations have encouraged the formation of such local non-profit sponsorship, particularly in the housing field and especially in the multi-family housing field.

Again, we face problems which are being worked on at the present time, but which have not been fully solved. Such local groups, in most cases, lack the technical know-how. How do you acquire a piece of land? How do you get financing for it? Where does the money come from? How do you hire the right architect? The right builder? The right urban planner? Who, in the parish, is qualified to do real estate management? If no one is available locally, how do you get the best outside man? How do you determine what the community really wants? Is the pastor of the church able to decide whether to build one-bedroom, three-bedrooms or five-bedrooms? Is he able to decide or is he qualified to decide whether to attempt § 221(d)(3) financing, rent supplement or a Turnkey Housing Program?

I have only touched on a few of the many problems faced by non-profit sponsorship groups. Vast efforts at all governmental levels and at the philanthropic level are being made to give these non-profit groups the money and technical skills necessary to solve these problems, but we have only begun to scratch the surface.

CONCLUSIONS ABOUT COMMUNITY PARTICI- PATION

There is no question that local minority communities are going to be consulted increasingly in multi-family housing. In deciding whether to take on a particular job, the developer must analyze the situation quickly and carefully before he gets too deeply involved. He must ask himself whether the community has developed an organization that speaks for it, so that when he gets a commitment from the organization, he can tell whether he has something that is morally binding or not.

He must determine in advance what he is going to do about "equality of opportunity" and minority participation, and if he commits himself to both of these, he must ask himself what the cost will be and who will pay it.

Finally, both the municipality and the contracting parties who deal with non-profit sponsor groups must be prepared to put in the extra time necessary in dealing with unsophisticated groups that are called on to make highly sophisticated decisions as to number of units, rental market, lay-out types, etc. It will take longer to deal with local non-profit sponsor groups, but if they are a factor in the community you are dealing with, you must have the time and patience to deal with them, and, if you are profit-motivated, you must find out how to pay for that additional time.

Imaginative builders have found simple, yet new ways to analyze the minority market. For example, in one case that we know of, a developer who could not decide on what the community really needed used that most famous of all middle-class housing developmental techniques—he built model apartments. Then, his 221(d)(3) prospects were able to help him in selecting lay-outs to meet their particular needs, to make suggestions on equipment in their apartments which the builder would never have thought of, and to remove some expensive items he otherwise would have felt were necessary. Armed with the results of questionnaires issued to his model apartment tenant prospects, he was able to get deviations in design specifications by his local FHA office.

If you know there is a problem, there is always a way to solve it. During the next twenty years, those developers who learn best how to solve the problems of the low income housing market will be able to carve out a big chunk of the anticipated 1-1/2 million new units per year.

INDEX

217